HEARING GOD'S CALLING

Dennis H. Hoyer

◆ FriesenPress

Suite 300 - 990 Fort St
Victoria, BC, Canada, V8V 3K2
www.friesenpress.com

Cover Photo by Lana Major

ISBN
978-1-4602-7639-6 (Hardcover)
978-1-4602-7640-2 (Paperback)
978-1-4602-7641-9 (eBook)

1. Biography & Autobiography, Religious

Distributed to the trade by The Ingram Book Company

Table of Contents

Endorsements

This is the story of one man's journey to God. It was fraught with peril and disappointment, but through it all God continually reached out to him. Through many trials the Heavenly Father brought him to a place of peace and inward joy, despite all the difficulties he endured. He became a better person rather than a bitter one and so can you.

No matter what the obstacles in your life the love of God is greater than any of them. He can and will deliver and restore you, if you look to Him. He and He alone is our rock, our salvation and our very great reward. Dennis found a balm of healing for his wounded soul in communion with Jesus Christ, and so can you. Jesus Christ is the healer of all broken hearts. *Joan Hunter President/Founder of Joan Hunter Ministries Canada Author/Evangelist*

Do you feel as if your life is in a total mess, you have been abused from your birth, you seem to be a destructive force in everything you do, you have no self-respect and are at your wits end? This is the book for you! Dennis lays out how his life was all of the above and how, despite all that, God loved him enough to make a direct intervention in his life and turn him 180 degrees around and placed him on a different path. This book may very well be God's intervention in your life and may help you to find the path to a more purposeful, peaceful, humble, and genuine life that God wants for you. A life filled with joy and the knowledge of God's love and plan for you. Take the time, read, reflect, and start your new life. Your journey has already begun, if you take the first step.

This book, despite all its painful details of the story of Dennis's life, is not about Dennis. It is about how Dennis's story (and ours) is part of the far bigger story of God's work in creation and God's providential, interaction, love and purpose for Dennis and for each of us.

The greatness of this book lies not in how a life off the rails was turned around by the determination of the author; but rather how despite the author's messed up life, God was able to intervene and transform a path to destruction, into a path to personal growth and the promise of eternal life.

Reverend Peter Boote

Rector Chinook Anglican Parish, Maple Creek, Sk.

Several years ago I came to know Dennis after my wife and I moved to a new community. His difficult life and experiences made him a desperate person for Christ's saving forgiveness, so when Christ touched his heart, he exploded in gratitude to his Lord. Whatever Jesus asks him to do he does it, without question, no matter the personal pain or the strange circumstances. He is an amazingly obedient follower of Christ Jesus.

Emeritus Pastor Terry Sauder
Canadian Association of Lutheran Congregations

Introduction

Upon writing this book, I found the main reason for writing the book was "What is love"? Now that this book is nearing completion, I ask myself what and how has this directed my life. At this moment, I am aware that it has definitely made an impact in my life. In so many ways I have a deeper understanding of myself, which are difficult to explain.

I am an incredibly supernatural being, divinely chosen.

God comes to us when we are hopelessly lost without Him.

To proclaim the Kingdom (The Gospel of Jesus Christ)

We all have a rap sheet soaked in blood. An exchange. Bad for good via the Cross.

To see others through the eyes of Jesus

"God opposes the proud, but He gives grace to the humble." James 4:6

I pray for fresh wisdom to keep me from theological arguments and not to weaken me in becoming lethargic. Amen

He hears my prayers

He sees my tears

He purchased me with His life.

He watches me as I toss and turn.

His wounds have paid my ransom.

It was my sin that held Him there.

All my life I struggled with who I was on a continual basis. I always keep a note pad in my pocket keeping tabs of things that touched my heart to keep me moving on. As I was tormented, I was searching how to dot the "I's" and cross the "T's". Now I am finding here and there that some of them are already being put together. For such a time as this.

After a while you learn the difference between holding a hand and a caring soul.

You learn love does not hold security. You begin to learn kisses are not contracts.

Presents are not promises and you begin to accept your defeats with your head up and your eyes open.

With grace - not the grief of a child, you learn to build all your roads on today, because tomorrow is too uncertain and futures have a way of falling down mid-flight.

When we risk sharing our real feelings we develop relationships of understanding and trust.

For we cannot really care or be cared for, love or be loved, and understood, unless we are willing to open our treasures of time, substance and self.

After a while you learn that even sunshine burns if you get too much.

So plant your own garden and decorate your own soul - instead of waiting for someone to bring you flowers.

I have learned I can endure, I really am strong, I really have worth. And God loves me so much.

I learn to learn that with those I have known throughout my life, every good-bye is a learning experience. When I meet Jesus in Heaven, then I will truly understand. AMEN

I say Thank You, God

Dennis H Hoyer

✝

Dedication

This book is dedicated to my late friend Bruce Leslie ("Les") Anderson. I became very close to Les during the last few months of his stay in the hospital.

Les was a true cowboy throughout his entire 91 years and was always in love with all aspects of the ranching lifestyle.

Les was a follower of Jesus Christ. He was a man of integrity, and he was also gifted with an exceptional sense of humour.

There was one area of life that troubled Les and caused him to cry himself to sleep many nights. He stated that he knew people who had chosen to go down the wrong road, and he felt that someday they would be sorry.

Les said, "I have done too little too late on the good side during my life." Then he said to me, "Now, Dennis, I am passing the torch to you, as you must now just tell them the Truth." (I was writing my book as he was saying this to me, and I am also aware that it was not a coincidence that this was taking place.)

See you soon in Heaven, Les.

Your friend in Christ,

Love, Dennis

Acknowledgements

Brenda is my wife, soul mate, and supporter. Because of Brenda's past experience, she presents a deep love for Jesus through her strong support and understanding of God's love for her. Brenda has dedicated many painstaking hours through prayer and understanding to the completion of this book.

Brenda has also observed me going through numerous times of anguish, confusion, and frustration in trying to understand this process.

Without Brenda's Christian-based encouragement and prayer, there is no doubt that this book would never have become a reality.

Blessings to you, Brenda, with my deepest gratitude.

Thank you. Dennis

Rev. Peter Boote and the late Mary Ann Boote

Peter has been my mentor over the past two and a half years. I met Peter at the back of the Anglican Church. We were chatting for a few moments, and then Peter gave me a tour of the church. He explained that this was going to be a healing church. I replied, "I am in with you."

Peter and his wife, MaryAnn, have stepped in beside me on my journey. It is a spiritual pathway that takes me not only to the door, but leads me through to the other side, where God abides.

Thank you Peter and MaryAnn for being my mentors.

Joan Hunter (Ministries)

Joan tells the stories of her life as a child. She was told that she would never amount to anything. There and then I was connected to her because my past was the same.

Joan has written many books and now runs a worldwide healing ministry with mercy and grace.

She has shown me that God does what He says He will do.

I have travelled to numerous cities in Western Canada, as well as to Haiti with Joan's ministry. She has instilled in me that I am something in Christ.

Thank You, Joan, for being my mentor. I am now able to work with the lost. Thank you, Jesus. Amen

Doris Bircham

Doris is a lady that I met at a cowboy poetry gathering about nine years ago. She is a cowboy poet and loves to write.

Doris is an upbeat person who loves people. She is friendly, kind, and supportive. When I ask anything of Doris, she is always willing to help and give guidance. Over the years, Doris has told me that I am a good storyteller, and that I should write a book.

Doris, I consider you a helpful friend and a mentor who has helped me to accomplish my dream of writing this book.

Thank you for your listening ear.

Dennis

Also a note of special thanks to **Blair and LeeAnn Brost, Gerald and Janice Sanderson,** and **Ross and Cammie Anderson,** who have been my friends, supported me in my walk with God, and encouraged me in striving to follow Jesus at all costs.

Also to **Ross and Claire Pollock** and Diamond C Cowboy Church for allowing Brenda and myself to be a part of the Cowboy Church prayer team, and for all the support you have given us. Thank you.

Purpose of this Book

I am writing this book to tell the story of the memories of my life from as early as I can recall them. Twenty years ago I collected facts for a family history book. This history of my father's side dates back 300 years. Twenty-three years ago, a dream revealed to me that I was to write a book about myself. So now is the time to do it.

Basically, this book has been written to allow God to entrench into my heart the truth of His Word and for me to explore how that fits into my character. It is my dream to have the opportunity to pray for anyone who requests and reads my book. My objective is to make this world a better place to live in because of what I have shared. Amen. Because I have no idea what love really is, and having not learned what love is during my childhood and into my adult years, the only real truth I know for sure is that Jesus LOVES me.

My intention is to tell the story of my life – what it was like, what happened, and what it is like now. I want to present my memoirs in a simple, forward manner for others to read. No matter how far down the scale of life you have travelled, there is hope. My prayer is that someone out there reads parts of this book, and that it will encourage him or her to develop a new mindset for a better life. God is always prodding everyone to do His will to bring about change.

My story at this point is so unbelievable, so unimaginable, that you may have difficulty believing it. As insane as my life was, I am not going to leave anything important out of it; nor am I going to embellish it.

The life events I describe are true and as I perceived them at the time. However, throughout this book, I have changed names, places, dates, and other identifying details so as to not single out others to cause pain.

My hope is to write another book in the future for lighter reading. God willing and if the creek does not rise.

There was no joy or laughter throughout my life. Also, I never got close to anyone. It was just as if I had been put through a meat grinder.

On a side note, I will say that I have made many mistakes in my life for which I am deeply sorry. I have no bitterness, no anger, no lack of forgiveness or resentment towards anyone. Many of my years were spent in turmoil. There is no way I am able to go back to fix or change anything. No one ever put a gun to my head to force me to do anything. I made all my own choices. I take full responsibility for all my actions and deeds.

Now, Jesus forgave me for all my sins when He died on the Cross. If that is not a fact, then the Bible is a farce. But I know it is not a farce, for I am living proof of that.

This is harsh, but true for me: "The truth will set you free."

God does not send anyone to hell; people make that choice.

God will give every human being every opportunity to accept or reject Jesus as their Lord and Savior and to follow Him during their lifetime.

It is simple: Ask, believe, and receive. Mercy and grace was given to you and me by Jesus on the cross 2000 years ago. It is free and unconditional. God gave (sacrificed) His only son for all mankind only because He loves you. The password to Heaven is "Thank you".

You can be with Jesus in Heaven for eternity or in hell in outer darkness with the devil. It is your choice.

A sin is a sin and all sins are forgiven through Jesus Christ. We have all sinned. For example: Have you ever said something that was untrue? Yes or no? If yes, you are a liar. Have you ever taken something that was not yours? Yes or no? If yes, you are a thief. Have you ever hated someone? Yes or no? If yes, you committed murder.

Are we now on the same playing field? I failed in all of the above.

Everyone Has a Choice

When Jesus comes into your life, healing will come, whether it is physical or emotional. There is a vacuum or space there that needs to be refilled. So what happens now? We look back and see what had filled that place, what kept us comfortable, and separated us from God. And now we must fill that place with God. He becomes our source of life. (So when your aches and pains are gone, what do you talk about?)

When I was seriously considering writing a book, there were many questions in my mind that needed to be answered. Being truly aware that I was listening to God, I found I really needed His help and guidance. My heart needed a solid answer before this task was to be undertaken. Starting from the beginning, a serious inventory had to be taken of my life to tell me who I was, as I would be sharing my life with others.

I am not a trained pastor with a degree of divinity. I only have on-the-job training, so to speak.

My Qualifications for Writing this Book

I wanted to write a book.

I am healthy.

I know who I am in Christ.

I am a positive person.

I started a book a few years back.

I have an abundance of life and practical experience.

At my age (74), I want to be of value and pay back what I can of what God has given me.

I have a beautiful house and home.

I am learning to write poetry.

I am learning to play guitar.

I love Jesus and am a born-again, spirit-filled Christian.

I do not smoke or drink.

I help others and care about them.

I am willing to learn.

I am a discerner. I listen and I hear.

I know that my children are heaven-bound.

I have a reasonable financial recourse with which to get by.

I am able to cook, do woodwork and photography, and am a lay minster.

I am a forgiven person.

I love my family.

Throughout my life there has been a constant search for the reality of God and His role in my life.

My prayer throughout this book is that you will be able to see God revealing Himself to you, so you can examine your own belief system – whether it is known or unknown – and ask Him to reveal His truth to you.

I pray you have a face-to-face encounter
with your loving Lord and Savior.

My cynical nature never allowed me to
examine and listen to that truth. Accepting
a supernatural miracle and to receive one
was difficult for me to understand.

I wondered how a guy like me could have
suffered so much and is now able to smile,
enjoy life to the utmost, and have peace
and joy with such an abundance of hope.

We are called to paint a picture of Jesus in
this dark world for others to see. Amen.
There is one, and only one, purpose remaining in my life, and that is to do my utmost
to lead someone to Jesus and nothing else.

My Christian Walk

This story is a basic outline of my life and contains numerous detailed events and stories.

As I share my story now, I am on my walk with Jesus.

I started drinking at age 8. When I left the family farm and joined the work world, my drinking increased. I wanted to cover the truth of the life I was living. I used alcohol to cover up a life that was totally repulsive and unacceptable to me.

My life was filled with anger, bitterness, revenge, demanding, lying, cheating, stealing, swearing, not caring, cantankerousness, denial, and abuse. These and other characteristics convinced me that there must be a change made in my character.

In 1983, I was sent to an alcohol treatment centre for a life skills course. The course started on a Sunday. I remember sitting on my lawn, waiting for my ride to Saskatoon for the course. My whole body was in breakdown mode. I was shaking, and my stomach was in knots.

When I was dropped off at the institute, I was met at the door and shown to my room upstairs. I was advised that supper was an hour away. While unpacking my belongings, I brought out a 40-ounce bottle of scotch, a 26-ounce bottle of vodka, and 2 bottles of wine. As I placed all these bottles on the table, I realized that I was in an alcohol treatment centre. Thinking it would not be a wise idea to get drunk in that place, I did not drink.

As a matter of fact, that was my first day of sobriety: April 27, 1983. I have not drank since. That was the start of my living a sober life. When I stopped drinking, I became a dry drunk. That means I had to live without booze. But living in this crazy world with the same old ideas, I had to rely on something else in my life in order to live without a liquid crutch. For me, that was insanity.

That course lasted for a week. I was learning how to live sober. Going to meetings actually gave me peace because people talked sense there and were friendly to me.

That was 32 years ago. I have learned many things about life since then.

Chapter One:
My Grandparents

I am starting my book by going back into my history to give you some insight into where my grandparents came from and how I fit into the picture. Included are a few short stories of my grandfather's life and his proposal letter to his girl (my grandmother). You will see how difficult it was for them coming into a new country. My Grandfather Hoyer gave the Church of England an acre of his land on which to build a church. My cousin said that my grandfather apparently ran a few services there. However, there was never any mention of him being a Christian, just a church-goer sometimes.

I did a complete family history twenty years ago. If there is someone who is interested in what and how I found my information, I would be glad to share it. However, this is all that will be shared at this time.

There may be another book written sometime in the future.

Grandfather and Grandmother Hoyer Ancestry

Richard Hoyer in the Canadian Passenger Lists, 1865-1885	
NAME:	Richard Hoyer
GENDER:	Male
AGE:	35
BIRTH YEAR:	about 1854
DATE OF ARRIVAL:	2 May 1886
VESSEL:	*Vancouver*
SEARCH SHIP DATABASE:	Search for *Vancouver* in the 'Passenger Ships and Images' database.
PORT OF ARRIVAL:	Quebec City, Quebec, Canada
PORT OF DEPARTURE:	Liverpool, England; Londonderry, Ireland
Source Information Ancestry.com. *Canadian Passenger Lists, 1865-1935* [database on-line]. Provo, UT, USA: Ancestry.com Operations Inc., 2010.	

Grandfather Hoyer immigrated to Canada on May 2, 1886. I only know of a few stories some old people told me that I am able to remember. When he was in Ottawa in about 1886, he played music on a grand piano for Queen Victoria on one of her visits to Canada – although this is not confirmed in history books. In winter, he worked on the railroad in Winnipeg, loading railway ties onto flat cars, and in summer, he moved west to British Columbia. He was a book-keeper in Leighton, B.C. for the railroad. As a hobby, he collected and dried butterflies and shipped them back to Germany. He was on the board of directors of the Winnetka School District when it became a school in the Northwest Territories. On Sundays, he preached in a church in Edenwold.

The following is an envelope and letter (which has been photocopied) that Grandfather wrote proposing marriage to Grandmother while she was still in Germany. She then came to Canada, and they were married. The old stories of Grandmother are that she was a very educated and proper "real lady" of the day.

(This is the original letter as it was translated from German to English. It has been left in the original state, and no spelling errors have been corrected.)

Nr. 6a
Edenwold, Sask.
March 22th, 1890

My dear bride!

Today my dear Kätchen. I got your lovable letter from the third of the month.

Finally, today I risk to address you with the confidential YOU; than out from the letter of today I take with certainty that you will be a fidelity wife to me. I'm immense sorry that you was afraid too early. But I can put myself in your situation very well. You would have waited timid and anxious on my finally answer. But dearest Kätchen, you can believe it me if I hadn't been acquainted to you and hadn't known so good what I have to except of you, never I would have taken up the interrup connection again. Now I have seen that you didn't forgot me yet, that you have forgiven my mistake and will help together with me to bear everything, I cann't do other thing, without to do a second mistake, than to say: come here, come at my side, work with me together, I will protect you and so God will make me lucky. I can presently offer not much, a parcel of landed property, what the greatest part of it is waiting on the plough, and a little house on it, not beautiful wether inside nor outside. But I've spent on it some beads of perspiration. Still I give you definitely declare that we both become to live in it more satisfied as in some nice furnished house. Space is in the small-est cabin for a lucky loving pair. Dear Kätchen I know precise what I have to expect of you. You have suffered some sad. You have had to resighn yourself in quite a few various proportions. You shall also settle in to these here, All the more as you now can potter and work for your-self. Up to now you have had to work for other on not to high salary. Once now work for you-self. Kätchen never I can forget when i moved there, you have all considerable arranged and on parting I feeled by your handshake that a heart beat for me. But I couldn' allowed to make you hope, I was dependent. Now I'm self-employed, even if under simple relations, I have risked once to knock timidly, if my Kätchen is angry to me or has forgotten me. And God thanks you have forgiven and are still good to me. You will bear everything with me, good and bad. On this way I can not say "she doesn't fit in to the relations of this country". Here is suitable each who put his whole heart into the object, and that make you. You don't shell longer roam about under stranger people and with worry and grief conquer a little place. Come here on my breast. I will protect and shield you and prepare you a nice home. I think now you will reasurred some a little and prepare for the voyage, all my letters I hope are in your hands. Nearly I have sent once a week. This of today now would be the last of them, I will send, unless your departure be delaied. Come to me as sonn as I'm thinking to you so much, at the evening when I put myself to bed, in the morning when I get up, wherever I am at once. Oh would be the time still here, when I can embrace you, give you the first kiss in love your mouth. Then will come over new leaf, courage and new strength with me. It is a disconsolate life I have had here so far, unless time and unless plan. Oh might I all of that repay plentiful to you what you will do for me, my love possessed you, every thing else stand by God. On His blessing is all situated.

Today on Sunday I will bring to end this letter. The thaw-wind is blowing outside but I'm sitting comfortable worm in the cottage and think of you my far sweetheart. I'm touch wood – except a lumbago which I have got by the vexisting cold weather – well and lively. On Friday I couldn't come to bed only with pains. Today I feel considerable better and I hope I can work again tomorrow. The influenza is also here still just broken out light. Nearly all of the settler have had it. I have spared of it. The news from Winnipeg seems to me excessive. Against that it shell occured there very strong at the shore.

Since last week we have thaw. In places the country is free of snow and the cattle is going at the pasture. The long timber I couldn't get therefor. But to get the short staffs was possible. I hope to have here all together two days later.

Constuction wood must to be get later after the cultivation.

After my calculation couldn't you get an answer of me before the 10th of the month. I have got your letter on 14th February and on 18th had Mr. Pastor Schnieder the letters for you and the both sides parents posted. Twenty days it needs at least a letter nowadays.

Don't make you bad thoughts my dear Kätchen as if I am angry with you because the long stopped answer. It comes earlier than I have waited for. I have only to thank you and to wait with patience – what I am without you? We are informed everytime about the proportions in Germany of the newspapers. In one respect I'm glad to be out of thiese relation Probably someone isn't there sure of his life. Here you find the quitest proportions, everyone have to do enough with himself. Who doesn't want to work has to bear the consequences. Nobody look after him even he die of starvation. Rebellioness and impertinences are all the most not tolerated. Who doesn't like it have to go.

Today I wanted to celbrate my birthday with a bottle of wine together with Mr.Michaelis. He will go away again for a prolonged period. Because the bad weather and my lumbago I have to give up the intension.

If you can bring us some bottles german Rhein-wine with you for to have something at our wedding dinner table. Also bring with you wine-glasses I have at home. Here it is very hardly to get wine, because the commerce with liquor is in the Northwest Territory forbidden. Wrap up the bottles good between your clothes.

Now feel good and don't make you bad thoughts, you will find a peaceful little place at my side and no might on earth can take it away from you.

Kind regards for your lovable relatives.

With everlasting love,

your bridegroom longing waiting for you

R. H O Y E R

Grandfather Hoyer passed away in 1926. Grandmother Hoyer passed away in 1927.

The Homestead - *Document explaining the location of buildings on the farm north of Edenwold*

My grandfather's original homestead was about one and a half miles south of Edenwold, but he later moved eight miles northwest of town. This was a temporary living quarters west of the farm on the other side of the bush. The house was a hole dug in the ground with short walls. The roof was made of logs, mud, straw, and sod. In the later years, boards and tarpaper were used. The walls were made from mud and straw and were two feet thick. It was warm in the winter and cool in the summer. As soon as they could, they built the farmhouse, moving into it in

1900. William Winkler helped them build the farm-house, who was my mom's dad. My parents, siblings, and myself moved in later and lived there from 1921 until 1970.

The main entrance on the south side was the summer kitchen, which was across the front of and attached to the main house. The lean-to was 6 feet high on the house side, 6 feet wide, and was sloped towards the 3 feet high exterior wall. The lean-to was about 25 feet long. I got the kitchen table, and my oldest son, Scott, now has it in his house.

In my time, there was a wood box in the kitchen used to store firewood.. A rain barrel was used to melt ice and snow as water storage for household purposes. There was a big wood stove which was used to bake bread and many meals. Other items in the kitchen were the washstand, radio, telephone, slop pail, and clothes rack.

Between the kitchen and master bedroom was the "little room", which held a couch, the china cupboard, a chair, the woodstove, a bread crock, and a three-drawer chest that my son Kim now has. Straight through the kitchen was the back bedroom, which was used for storage. In the sixties, it was remodelled for Grandmother Winkler to live in.

Off to the left of the little room was a large bedroom. In it was the writing desk (my son Kim has it), an old table, a dresser, and the baby crib where my sister Linda slept. On the north wall was a big clothes closet. In the corner was a high chest of drawers that I still have.

On the east wall was Mom and Dad's bed; my brother and I slept at the end of their bed. On the south wall was a storage cupboard. Beside our bed was a round wood stove.

On the east side of the bedroom was a room called the (lean-to) backroom. In early years, I think it was used for hired men to sleep in.

The Root House "Cellar"

The root house was located approximately 75 yards northwest of the house, halfway to the ice house. The front had six large steps down to the cellar. The root cellar was approximately 40 feet wide by 80 feet long, with eight-foot ceilings, divided in half. The walls were made of cement and had an arched roof that was 3 feet thick with two vent holes. It was dug into the side of the hill and covered with manure, dirt, and grass.

The cellar was divided into two sides. The east side contained approximately 80 to 100 bags of potatoes, carrots packed in sand, turnips, parsnips, mice and lizards!!!

On the west side were shelves of canned goods – approximately 50 to 100 quarts of corn, peas, Saskatoon berries, pears, peaches, etc. There were also stone crocks of sour cabbage (sauerkraut). By late fall, the place was completely full of food and ready for winter.

Beside the house there was what we called the wash shack. Inside the shack were the washing machine and a stove. The washing machine was powered by a one-cylinder Cushman engine. Water had to be carried from the well or ice and snow was melted to wash clothes. Later the Cushman engine was used to pump water at the well, and a small Brigs and Stratton engine was used to wash clothes.

The Tool Shack and Other Structures

The tool shack was located south east of the house and beside it was a 6-foot by 6-foot by 8-foot oil shack. The tool shack held numerous types of tools and equipment. There also was a forge and anvil, which I have. It was really a blacksmith shop. I enjoyed it because I would light the coal and turn the crank and make the coals turn red. Then I would place an iron in it until it became red-hot. Then the iron was hammered into a shape on the anvil. We sharpened plows, shears, cultivator shovels, etc. The material was dipped into water in small spurts to temper the steel. I used to make a little money in the fall from doing blacksmith work to pay for hunting licenses, shells, etc., on request by the neighbors.

There were also other buildings on the farm that had various uses. Just north of the tool shack was a tar-paper shack that was used as a chicken house. It was a neat building and was originally used for threshing crews to sleep in.

Just north of the tar shack (chicken house) was another large structure made of mud, straw, and logs. The west side was the smaller portion, and the east side was the larger portion. One side housed poultry, the other side housed pigs. The whole farm set up was very advanced for the time.

East of the chicken/pig barn was the shed (red with white trim). It had a very large west side and long east side. The large side was used to store the threshing machine, the other side was for other farm implements.

A little south of the red shed was the well. The well had excellent hard water, suitable for drinking, and there was lots of it. I do not ever remember it not supplying the humans' and animals' requirements plus the other needs for water on the farm.

South of the well was the barn. It was large in the middle with a low portion expanding to the west and east. The center part was a hayloft, chop (for cattle and horses), the general feed supply, and the calf pens.

The Ice House and Smoke House

There is no picture of the ice house, so I drew a picture of it as I remember it as a child.

The ice house was located in the bush, approximately 150 yards northwest of the main house.

The building was constructed of 8-inch to 10-inch diameter logs and filled with mud and straw. The roof was the same except it had dirt with grass (sod), which kept out the weather. In the summer, it was a very cool place to keep the food.

The ice house was constructed over a cement hole, which was approximately 15 feet by 15 feet square and

20 feet deep. There was a 2-foot ledge around the hole next to the log walls.

The front portion was the smoke house. That is where the cured ham, bacon, and sausage were smoked for a few days and then left to hang. The meat would be left in there in the summertime as the flies would not touch it as it was kept cool from the ice and heavy log walls. The hams were injected with a special salt brine and soaked in big wooden barrels filled with brine solution in the root cellar before smoking.

Usually about the end of January or the beginning of February, the hard task of filling up the ice house began. The task took six days, and we hauled two loads of chipped ice per day. Two horses, Barney and Lucy, were harnessed and hitched to the sleigh and wagon box. Dad, my brother Ronald, and myself would chip the ice with an ice pick and load it with a shovel. I was fascinated at how Dad could drive to the ice house and back the horses and sleigh to the front of the ice house. The ice was shoveled off the sleigh box and hurled onto a couple of planks so it could slide into the ice hole.

Twelve sleigh boxes of ice were put into the ice house hole and covered with straw. The ice was used for making ice cream or for keeping cream, butter, and other food items cool. The containers were lowered with ropes in later summer as the ice level went down. It was used as a refrigerator.

Over the years, all of the farm has disappeared. Only a sad, falling-down mud house and the cellar remain as landmarks of what used to be. While writing this book, my mind seemed to visualize and dream what it was possibly like in those days.

One time a few years ago, I drove into an abandoned prairie town only two hours from where I live. In the middle of the street was a lonely old pump and stand. I took a photo of it and then wrote a poem (see "Fir Mountain" below) about how I thought it might have been in days past. The poem "Heartfelt Expression" below explains the very reason that I have included my poetry in this book.

Heartfelt Expression

For me poetry reveals deep

feelings and emotions

That are too intense for me to express

And to get them into the open

They are splattered in my heart.

It is a way I am able to reveal

Just how much God's creation

Can inspire my life.

Fir Mountain

Ribbons of steel brought settlers to Fir Mountain

Clanging bell, steam hissing, whistle blowing

Foreign passengers at the train

station tugging their trunks

Gathered for a moment gratitude
their hearts were singing.

Dry hot sun rose concern that water was vital
Men gathered shovels, pails
inducing piles of earth
When water was struck,
elation spread amongst all
Located centrally a village, with
a well, now gained worth.

Black steel pump stood boldly on its perch
Water desperately required for quality of life
Long pump handle would
suck water from a pipe
All parts function well, bringing no strife.

Many deep long strokes
were needed for the prime
Young folk hardly grasped the top on tiptoe
Banging, squeaking, some water gushed
Soon tin pail was partially full,
oh I wish I would grow.

Throughout the day school children pass by

Girls sat, giggling about

friendships lasting forever

Boys shouted, wrestling,

throwing rocks with energy

All felt secure, safe with dreams ending never.

Late hazy summer afternoon mom calls dinner

Kids take different trails home with jeans torn

Carrying a pail of splashing

water for dinner dishes

Entering the door receiving a face

wash from mom's apron.

Days, years, pass as family memories grew

Surrounding pump stand

provided a seat of solace

Town folk routinely walked by

for their water supply

Families converge on an evening

stroll at a calm pace.

Still moonlight casting its black images

Windows open, for fresh air while resting

One last peek downtown, all was at peace

Old pump piercing fading

blue sky line not testing.

Time was to blow out the

coal oil lamp in smoky chimney

Old Rex circled near the bed that was his place

Croaking frogs echo their song from wet marsh

Exhausted grateful eyes close

with heartfelt grace.

Passing on that abandoned road

now, one would hardly notice

It stands proudly amongst tall

weeds with sour pill

Vibrant homes once displayed love

are gone, only vacant lots

Seasons pass, sun rises and sets, the pump is still.

—DENNIS H. HOYER

Grandmother Winkler

Grandmother Winkler was my mom's mother. She was always very kind, full of fun, and full of stories.

After she sold the farm, she moved to Regina, and then eventually to Lumsden. She lived with my aunt and uncle. After my uncle sold his farm in about 1947, my grandmother came to live on our farm. The back storage room was cleaned and fixed up and made into a nice bedroom.

Grandmother was ill and somehow got into a county hospital because of gallstones, but complications set in, and she died there.

Throughout my history on both sides of my family, to my knowledge, church and faith were not in the forefront of their lives.

All my family on both sides never seemed to share anything personal about themselves or the past.

Grandfather Winkler passed away on October 18, 1940. Grandmother Winkler passed away in 1970.

I searched my soul endlessly for years to know who in my family would have ever prayed for me. It is only recently with new information that I believe my Grandmother Winkler did because she was raised Baptist.

She was a kind, loving person. Grandmother had six daughters and one son.

I am sure my mom and dad also prayed for me, however, they never ever shared any of it with me.

My grandmother was the only one of my grandparents that I got to know somewhat.

Chapter Two:
Memories of My Dad

My dad was born in 1899 in a log and mud house that was built over a dug out on the side of a hill. The house was sheltered by a bush of poplar trees on three sides to protect it from harsh weather.

I was born in 1940, and I lived on this farm till I was 15. That is where Grandfather and Grandmother Hoyer had lived with three sons and one daughter. My dad (Max) lived there all his life until his death in 1970. He went to school for three terms, for three years in July and August to get his grade three.

When I was doing my homework one night in the kitchen under the gas lamp, Dad was in a chair a few feet away, sound asleep. He was awakened by my grumbling about working on a solution for an algebra question. Dad said, "What is the matter with you?"

I was crying because I did not know how to solve the problem.

Dad just looked at it and gave me the answer. The next day, my teacher asked how I got the answer. I said my dad gave it to me. Then there was trouble again.

Dad never went through the procedure; he just knew the answer.

Dad never talked much. He was very gentle, worked hard day and night, and never worried about anything.

His favorite saying was "ach", meaning "never mind".

I never ever heard Mom and Dad talk, there was only arguing or grumbling.

My dad loved to sit and eat ice cream.

One summer there was a severe hailstorm. Mom gathered the hailstones, which were the size of a quarter, and made pink ice cream. I was excited, but my dad was crying. I figured it out many years later. He was crying because his crop was gone!!!

One time, in late fall, my dad was repairing his combine in the late afternoon. A neighbor walked over to the field and asked my dad to come to his place. He needed help to get his tractor started. Dad said, "Sure". He walked over to help him, and that night it snowed and he never got his crops in.

My dad was not ambitious. One day ran into another. Dad never had any money. When Dad died, we three kids sold some cattle to pay the debt on the land that had been left by Grandfather.

We went to church once in a while in the summertime. The women sat on the left side of the church and the men on the right. During the service, my mom made me sit beside Dad to poke him when he fell asleep.

Dad always said grace in German. Even though dad never said much, it seemed to be the right thing for him to do.

Dad was poor and humble, and was a very easy going man, with no worries. One day just went into the next.

My feeling is that Grandfather Hoyer left my dad with such a large debt load, that he feared he would never get out of it. Someone in the family said that Mom and Dad were told by my Grandfather Winkler to walk away from it all, and that he would help them get started somewhere else. But dad said, "No!" My dad would never ask anyone for help.

My dad was always calm, and he never gossiped.

One summer Saturday night while in town, it began to rain. On the way home, it began to pour. Our Model A Ford car used to have a canvas roof on it. However, for some reason it was missing. We as a family were getting totally soaked. When we arrived home, Dad lit the barn lantern and went into the kitchen.

As the house was made of mud and logs, the wind blew the roof off the top. Rain soaked the mud ceiling. There was a foot of mud on the kitchen table plus lots on the floor. Mom just exploded, screaming and totally out of control. Mom left the house and ran away in the rainy darkness.

Dad noticed she had taken the shotgun with her. Dad just told us kids to go to bed, which the rain also completely soaked. Dad just cleaned up the mess and was not upset at all. He was a very steady man.

My dad sat at the head of the table to my right. One time I was screaming and complaining that I did not like what was on my plate at suppertime. My dad, with his left hand, swung and hit me. I hit the floor as he said, "You eat what is on your plate or go to the back room (where I slept) for the night. Your plate with the food shall be on the table in the morning." And it was, and I ate it. I never complained again, and I can eat almost anything. That is the only time Dad ever disciplined me.

Now when I go on mission trips to Mexico and Haiti, I eat all foods. Food is scarce for them and not always good food to say the least.

The routine of the day was waking up in the morning, going to the bathroom, having something to eat, getting on the buggy, and then riding two and a half miles to school.

Often while sitting in my desk, I would be looking out the window, dreaming about playing cops and robbers during recess time. I was not learning anything because I was not listening.

There was nobody to talk to at school or at home. I just was alive. I had no purpose. There was no one that cared about me. I had no communication with anyone. I just had myself and my daydreams.

At this point in time, I am wondering where the end of this book is going to take me. No one but God knows the outcome.

My Prayer: In the name of Jesus, please be with me to give me the wisdom and direction required of me that only you can do. As my understanding is so limited in your creation, let my heart, mind, and soul hear your wisdom and will as I share my life. Please dear Lord, let the truth be spoken here, let the truth be heard here. Thank you, Jesus.

One experience was when my dad was planting a crop on the north quarter with four horses and a seed drill. I must have been three or four years of age when I walked a half a mile to see my dad. My plan was to run up behind the seed drill and get on the walking plank. Then I would be able to go a few rounds with my dad. My dad never paid any attention to help me up. I would just about get to the rear of the drill, my hands would slip off, and I would fall to the ground. My short legs would scramble hard in the loose, stony, dry, and dusty dirt. Falling face down, my eyes would be full of dust as well as my mouth. This routine took place three or four times while I was screaming and crying in frustration. Finally giving up, I went home.

To continue the previous story, my dad and I went out to the southwest quarter after supper on a nice harvest moon night with a team of horses. We loaded the hayrack wagon with oat sheaves and were now homeward bound. While we rode home, I was laying on top of the swaying load watching the stars. The harvest smell was in the cool air. The horses' hoofs on the hard road were making clip-clopping sounds, and I could hear the jingling harness and the metal wheels grinding on the road. My day ended watching the North Star and the Big and Little dippers. Dad explained that about 60 miles north there were two sets of town lights. I told myself that I would visit those towns when I grew up. However at this point, I have not been able to go there.

Chapter Three:
My Mom

Pondering

We all see in others in their imperfection

Soft gentle breezes wisp through our souls

Dreaming of heavenly thoughts

because of our perfection

Being aware, anything against love is sin.

If a buried bulb can grow to be a flower

If an egg can become a bird to soar and sing

Why doubt the resurrection of power

Of the risen King.

Pines standing on the ocean shore

Reaching, stretching, learning

from the rock under

That it is able to swing and

sway, talk with the sky

Becoming mindful that there

is no need to wonder.

I am a person who has

developed life's battle scars

Searching for assurance of God's perfect pick

With every seed that is planted and growing

I may never see the result on the end of a wick.

Rusty dust rising high for a rainbow to digest

Beauty appears through

spraying of splendour faze

Rising towards a bright warm light

Hand brushed by the painter, for his praise.

Stormy days are past, while feeling love

Watching clouds fleeting by is not wasting time

We cast our shadow standing

in our own sunlight

Every good dream begins with a great dream.

—DENNIS H. HOYER

My Mom

This story about my mom, that is forthcoming, is really the pivotal part of this book. For me, it is very sad and extremely difficult to write about. This story has been in my heart for most of my life. In this last year, I have read about six books on how to write a book. Well, at this point there were many suggestions on how to present my emotions and *to not do* this or that, but *to do* this and that. The best book I read was called *If You Can Read You Can Write*.

I finally decided to just write, because I had no idea how to put my thoughts on paper for you, the reader, so that you could understand me and I could still stick to the truth.

So this is my story. For me it is the truth even though there are plenty of people who would totally disagree with me. It took me twenty-nine years to get a grip on this story. It is beyond my comprehension how and why this all could have taken place.

My prayer and hope in getting this story on paper is that the reader and I will be able to get to some resolution and believe there is a loving God in Heaven and He is hearing my plea. God is looking from the balcony of Heaven, dispatching His angels right now to show us His grace and mercy that lets us know He cares. His heart was broken many times throughout my life because of the way I was living my life.

My mom had many good qualities, which I will detail through this story. Most of her life while raising me, it seemed to be a real challenge for her, and in doing so, anger, bitterness, and resentment was the daily menu toward me. I never, ever heard my mom and dad talk. They just grunted and fought. Nor do I ever remember going to Mom to get consoled or her offering a listening ear.

In my life, I was aware that I was to be beaten. I just never knew why or when or how much and with what. It seemed no matter what I did or thought, or how hard I tried to avoid it, I got beaten. I had scars on my back from whatever Mom was able to get a hold of – a willow switch, razor strap, stove poker, her hands, or blocks of wood.

I just accepted, breathed air, and carried on.

I learned to pick Saskatoon berries, plus many other berries, cut wood in the bush, hauled it out, sawed it, and split it up.

One time, Mom grabbed the wood stove poker and beat me. I flew against the hot stove, cutting my lip and forehead. I was bleeding, but Mom left crying and went to bed.

Mom was a large woman. When she was outside in the yard, she would find a willow switch or whatever she could get her hands on and beat me. At the age of 14, Mom could not catch me or handle me, and the beatings slowly stopped.

However, if I would run away, things went really bad when I got back to the house. We had lots of screaming matches. I figured out a system because she was a heavy person. I would run circles around her, playing her out, then let her catch me. My reasoning was that I would receive three to four swats instead of ten.

We had a neighbor who lived about a mile to the west of our yard. I am sure that he heard my screams because once he asked me what was going on over there. I said, "I was a bad boy."

I am also sure he told other neighbors of my dilemma because the neighbors let me hunt and trap on their land. Also, several neighbors would bring all kinds of blacksmith work to me so I could earn some money to go hunting and buy trapping supplies.

One time, Mom was chasing me. I probably was about 6 years old. Mom caught me beside the woodpile. Mom grabbed me and threw me to the ground, held me down on the ground, and stood on me. She grabbed a log of wood and pounded me on the head many times. To get away from all the abuse, I would go into the surrounding poplar bushes for the day and just lie there watching the fleecy clouds float by. My dog Sparky would lie beside me and keep me company.

I believe that in those early years of development, my spirit broke away from people. I had no connections. I did seem to always have compassion for people from a distance. I will always help people with whatever and whenever. However, it seems when the rubber hits the road, most people just watch me and attempt to figure me out.

I would like to mention that as of this time, January 2015, I have had the privilege of leading many people to Jesus. Because of my former years, God has conditioned me to do what I am supposed to do, lay hands on the sick, cast out demons, and raise the dead.

This part of my story will be told in detail later in this book.

As I had experience with the Lord, it started to get me on the right road.

I will not hold you in suspense. I led my mother to Jesus and was at her bedside when she went home to be with the Lord. She had a smile on her face. Praise to Jesus, amen.

This insert will explain how years later, after I had gone for treatment, I visited my mom at her home many times. Together we talked about her childhood. Something that I said caused her to explode, telling me, "You have no idea what it was like. When my dad came home from the beer parlor drunk, he chased Mom around the hayrack with an axe in front of all of us children..." Well, I listened and heard what had brought her to this place in her life.

My parents did the best they could, living back in the bush, with no connections with others.

I always felt that I was the most ugly and stupid person in the world, so I never strived to be loved and accepted through my distorted image of people.

My mother had a sense of humor in a small crowd. Mom cooked at a church camp at the lake. While at a camp service, the pastor was giving the closing remarks. Mom stood up to hear him preach and threw a pail of water on him. What applause!

As crazy as all this may sound, I have a difficult time recalling my memories of the past. Because of that, it was hard getting going on this project.

I do not remember having any type of discussion of any sort with my parents during my childhood. There was only grumbling, silence, and arguing. There was no laughing, peace, or a sense of contentment or happiness. There was always an order to shut up and go to work.

My mother as usual, ignored me, always siding with my brother. I always received the same treatment, a beating for lying. In those days, the eldest son was it, he had the say in all matters.

All my past was stress. Having many sessions of counselling from age 20 to 68 has left a sour taste in my mouth. After two weekends, two years apart in my Ancient Paths Seminars (it is a seminar that helps you to find out about your past), the question always came back to me: Where was Jesus when my mom was pounding that block of wood on my head? Finally, I began to realize that He was down on the ground beside me because He felt all my pain. That was the turn around. I then was able to forgive my mom.

At Present

My mom said many times after my
beatings while I was hiding under the
bed, "God will get you for this", as she
continued to instill fear into me.

I figured it out just lately.

God has me now. He always will have me.

Jesus was a carpenter. (I am a woodworker.)

I am a Stephen minister.

I am a personal introduction agent.

All because Jesus died on the Cross at Calvary
for all my sin. I am forgiven. Amen.

Everything against love is sin.

You either love someone or hate them.

I have a saying: "Place one foot ahead of
the other and your butt will follow."

Chapter Four:
My Childhood

Butchering a Rooster

One morning, Mom made an announcement that company was coming for dinner. I was told to help surround and capture two roosters for dinner. Two were brought to an open space of the barnyard. Mom commanded me to hold one rooster while she took the other one. Standing on the spread wings with the head over a log, whack, she used the meat cleaver like a guillotine. The lifeless head lay on the ground. Then the rooster was thrown into the air with its wings flapping. It fell on the ground, and then propelled itself three feet in the air. Blood was squirting in all directions. Mom grabbed the other rooster from me and repeated the procedure. This was a very dramatic scene for one of my young age.

Now there were two beheaded roosters airborne in all directions. I was scared, terrified, and screaming in horror. I was covered in blood and started running to and fro, attempting to escape this evil adventure. There was no escape. I made a dash with a rooster hot on my trail. Barefooted, I spun out on a fresh cow paddy. Falling face down in the dirt, one rooster ran right over to me. I had nightmares for weeks on end. No one pulled me close to speak softly to me while I cried and screamed hysterically.

The dogs enjoyed eating the heads of the roosters. Just like candy.

First Day of School

It was cool on the first day of September

Time to pull up the bib overhauls

Lunch pail, Kool-Ade, apple,

and Spam sandwiches

Through two gates, a creek, the Model A crawls.

Two and a half miles on a bumpy road

I stare at the school not knowing what to think

Neighbors came with cars and

buggies with children

Cream can filled with water

that was cool to drink.

Moments pass, school marm rings opening bell

Classroom appeared large,

I was shown to my seat

English language was different than mine

Insecurity runs deep into my trembling feet.

Introduction, regulations and rules

Tears came to my eyes, I am

saved by the recess bell

Outside people came over to say welcome

Cops and robbers, first base,

kick the can and baseball.

Step by step the ordeal became normal

Corn broom, dust pan, I swept

the rough floor with care

Homeward bound, cows found and milked

Family supper, play, romp with dog then prayers.

—DENNIS H. HOYER

Good Morning to a Regular School Day

A regular school day in winter was something else. Dad got up about 5:30 a.m. to start the fire on the wood cook stove in the kitchen. Then he started a pot of rolled oats for breakfast.

When a frigid winter storm was howling from the south with vengeance, snow would get through the space between the wood frame and mud wall. There was a six-inch wide strip of snow drift which came 8 feet up to the bed.

When the call came from Dad to rise and shine for breakfast, I swung out from under the covers. My feet landed on the flange of the wood space heater, and I quickly got my felt boots on.

The bathroom, which consisted of a pail with a seat on it, was located off the bedroom in a board-covered lean-to.

Oh yes, the seat was frost covered, and there was news and catalogue paper for butt wipe. At Christmas we were blessed with the paper wraps from the Christmas oranges. I cannot believe to this day that I was so blessed to have such comfort.

After breakfast, Dad had the school pony harnessed and hooked up to the cutter. We sat on an oat sheave holding onto a lunch pail under a blanket. Then off we went two and a half miles to school.

At school, the furnace there had to be stoked up to make the classroom comfortable and suitable for a day in school.

Babe – My School Pony

She was a wily, fence-jumping, brown mare
Who pulled our buggy to school each day.
Babe was her name, her strong will was a flame
Causing many a wreck and runaway.

She loved to race with other school rigs
Tongue flashing, teeth clicking on steel bit
Neck cranked high with glassy eyes
Leather harness covered with foam to show grit.

Racing started on the way home from school
Through the gate, flat out for over a mile
Brother Ron, on the reins,
crossing over a dry slough
I flew out, broke my arm, Babe won in style.

Saturday was a day of cold winter trapping
Rope around the collar, to toboggan on the line
Muskrats, weasel, and mink were the catch
Furs prepared, taken to town
for money that was mine

Sunday Dad said, "Babe must have a day of rest."

We kids had to walk a few miles

Dugout hockey was extremely important

Babe was in stall content with a sneer and smile

—DENNIS H. HOYER

Winter Travel to School by Horses – 1947 to 1948

That winter was extreme. The snowdrifts were as high as the telephone lines, approximately 15 feet deep.

As this was my first year of school at 7 years of age, my dad took my brother and myself to school with a horse and sleigh. Halfway to school, the team of horses broke through the deep snow. I remember my dad trying to settle the team down. The horses were rolling in the deep snow screaming while tangling themselves in the harness as my dad quickly shoveled to get them out so we could leave. It was quite a horrifying experience for me.

Trip to Regina on a Steam Train – 1947 to 1948

During the winter of 1947 to 1948, my dad took me to the train station 8 miles away by horse team and sleigh. Why? I have no idea. Maybe it was to see a dentist or eye doctor? I just do not remember. Dad left me at the station with the station agent to look after me. All this was all so new to me. That winter there were snow banks as high as 20 feet. On the train, peering out the scratched frost-covered window of the passenger car, all that was to be seen was the steam coming from the train engine past my window. As the snowdrifts were so high, the steam came past the car, leaving no room between the train and the snowdrifts.

Once at the platform of the train station in Regina, panic set in as I began walking amongst all the people, luggage carts, and freight. I was overwhelmed by the endless platform, the people, the very cold temperature, the steam that seemed to have no end in sight, – and all the strange noises. I was just pushed into the flow of people in the train station. I had no idea where I was going. No one told me what was going on. I have no idea how I got to my grandmother's house.

The next day, I went to the doctor's office by taxi. After that, I was in the Broadway Theatre watching Roy Rogers.

Going through all these situations, what could happen next?

The movie was the first one I had ever seen. I was totally smitten, and I was glued to the screen.

Now the real story gets into full swing. I had to go to the bathroom and had no idea where it was. By the time I found a restroom and removed some clothes, all hell broke loose. Well, you guessed it, I crapped my pants. I mean it gushed out all over my clothes and legs. Now what? I was missing the movie. I was crying and yelling for help in the basement with no one to come to my aid.

I cleaned myself up the best I knew how and got back to see the rest of the show.

Once again, I went back to Grandmother's house. I never told her what had happened. I slept under a blanket on the chesterfield for the night. Because of guilt and shame, not a word was mentioned about my accident. I had breakfast and then went back to the train station for the ride home. Then it was eight miles by horse and sleigh in freezing winter weather. It was three days before bath night and back to school by horse cutter.

Now bath night was in the kitchen, beside the wood stove. I was third in line for a bath. When one person finished their bath, a few gallons of water were dipped out, poured into a large kettle, and warmed up on the stove for the next person.

My brother and my dad were next.

My butt was so sore.

I was crying. That bath felt so good. Locating some Vaseline in the cupboard, I lathered myself up so I would be able to sleep the whole night. I was questioned by Mom for months about the missing pair of underwear as I only had two pairs of them. I never told Mom that I had buried them under the snow in the bush.

Drinking at Age 8: A Pivotal Moment

With all of the confusion in my life, there was a pivotal moment that took place when I was eight years of age. I remember telling a story to a few people that I wanted to be a minister or a carpenter.

One evening, my parents had company. They had come to our place for an evening of card playing. They were playing cards in the kitchen. I was alone and playing in the other rooms of the house in the darkness while in my own little lonely world.

All anyone really wants is to be loved and accepted.

Mom had a large clothes closet with doors on it. Upon entering the closet, I found it was a very safe place to be. No sounds, very cuddly, and alone. Working around amongst the clothes and shoes, I came upon a bottle. I remember fiddling around, opening the bottle, and then smelling it. It had such a wonderful, soothing smell. As no one would ever find me there, I was free to do whatever I wanted. I lifted up the bottle to my mouth, taking a good gulp of its contents. I felt a smooth, comforting fluid flowing into my mouth, down through my stomach, and into my veins. I had found my answer to all my life problems. It instantly left me feeling safe and secure and at peace. That cherry whiskey now had a grip on my life. This road I travelled for 35 years.

Babysitting Mrs. Homersham – 1949

My neighbor was a bachelor. In the early years, he lived on the farm with his mother. His mother was 80 years old and had Alzheimer's. This lady could not be left alone for too long. One day I was asked to sit with her and keep her company while he worked in the fields. This lady was born and raised in London, England. Well, she had books and photos of London. She would flip through the books and read the stories over and over again.

I loved the stories about the London Bridge and the Tower of London that had taken place over centuries of time.

My neighbor often hired me to help fix the fence and drive the tractor on the binder at harvest time. He would also let me hunt and trap on his land and shoot gophers, rabbits, etc.

Skating at the Neighbors' – 1950

During the long, cold winters, I had to be creative about how to entertain myself. Sometimes my brother and I would walk two and a half miles south to the neighbors' and play ice hockey. Dad said that we could go, but the school pony had to rest so we had to walk.

When I went to school, for extra events, I took a willow branch and bolted two boards together to make a hockey stick. Now I had a hockey stick and a puck, which was usually a frozen horse turd.

Some other kids in the surrounding area also came. We all had shovels and cleaned off the dugout ice surface to play hockey. We played for a couple of hours. Then we had some hot chocolate, and we walked back home while soaking wet.

Repairing the Farm Water Pump

Water is always an essential commodity. Pigs, cattle, and horses got their water supply from a creek or slough. That was all season. However, in winter there was a well with a hand pump to draw the water to the top for domestic use as well as for the animals. Every few years, maintenance to the pump was required. With a block and tackle, the pump and pipe were drawn out of the well using a pole tripod. The well itself was about 3 feet in diameter, and it was approximately 50 feet to the water level. After new felt washers were replaced in the pump cylinders, it was lowered down back into the water.

While this procedure was taking place, I was amazed, while looking down the well cribbing. There were planks lying around the well opening for me to sit on. Focusing into the darkness and down to the water at the bottom of the well, I observed a mirror, glassy surface fifty feet below. After a few moments, the water was forming ripples. Again in shock, I observed two gophers swimming in the water in circles.

Really, my goodness, this is where the family got the drinking water from? Those gophers could die, rot, and spoil the water. I called Dad, explaining my findings to him and what I thought could be done about this.

"How could this be?" I asked.

Dad's answer: "DO NOT TELL MOM."

A Trip to Town with the Model A

Early Saturday afternoon, cows milked
Cream separated from milk, placed on ice
Calves, chicken plus pigs all served their feed
Supper was complete of
sauerkraut, chicken, and rice.

Tin bathtub on the floor, kettle on the stove
Stove damper closed, wood box full
Dressed in overhauls, we rushed to the Model A
Mom came last, giving the front
door a tug and a pull.

Gurgling and groaning down a country road
Once in town we went separate ways
Oh Henry, Orange Crush, oh yes, ice cream too
After a few hours, we gather,
home time, Dad says.

Thunder lightning, gale winds begin to swirl
Down pouring rain allows only
a glimmer of 6-volt lamp
21' spoked wheels eagerly hug sloppy ruts

Car roof now gone, only sky and

water makes me damp.

Our mud shack shows up with tarpaper gone

Smokey lantern shows a place I do not want to be

My bed soaking wet, I am tired and confused

I want to leave here and go back to the Model A.

—DENNIS H. HOYER

What I Did for Entertainment as a Kid

Evenings and weekends, I would take my dog Tobi and my rifle and go hunting bush rabbits to a slough north of the farmhouse that was surrounded with poplar and willow trees.

My dog loved this adventure for the next couple of hours. Tobi would scamper in and out of the trees, scaring the rabbits out. The rabbits would follow the trees around the slough. I set up in the bush, and as the dog chased the rabbits right past me, I would pick them off. Then I would go off to the butcher shop where I would receive up to twenty-five cents apiece for them.

Basically, I would just wander around the fields and trees hunting, just to get away from the abuse in the house. Nature, my dog, and God gave me some semblance of life and love.

Berry Picking, Gardening, Canning

Springtime was filled with planting a couple of acres of corn, peas, carrots, beets, onions, beans sweet peas, potatoes, parsnips, turnips, tomatoes, cabbage, cucumbers, dill, plus many other wonderful vegetables.

Now there was hoeing and keeping the weeds at a minimum in the garden.

Next it was Saskatoon berry picking, along with raspberries, choke cherries, blueberries, and goose berries as well.

Fall was harvest time. One cannot fill the cellar alone. The sides of the walls were about 40 feet wide and 60 feet long. One half of this area was shelves, which were filled with canned food until the next year. I mean 100 of these were one-quart sealers and two-quart sealers. The other side held anywhere from 100 to 125 bags of potatoes.

There were boxes full of carrots, parsnips, etc., buried in sand to preserve them. Just before winter set in, the door of the cellar was forced shut. A blanket covered the bottom of the door to prevent cold air from getting in and freezing the produce. It really was a nice home for lizards.

Now our food supply was safe.

Olle' Kamellen

The following entry has been passed down through the generations on my mother's side. These were smart and funny answers to whatever the situation might have been. Adults shared them back and forth, and the children quickly learned them and joined in the fun. Cultural wit at its best!

The language was called PLAUTDEUTSH in German, which was used in the Winkler family.

1. Whoever gets up early, God will honor.
2. A long thread – a lazy girl.
3. Pretty on the outside, but dirty on the inside.
4. When the time comes, there will be a solution.
5. The morning hour has gold in its mouth.
6. More haste – less speed.
7. If I do not come today, I will come tomorrow.
8. Once you have told a lie, even though you tell the truth, no one will believe you.
9. Save up early and you will have something in the future.
10. When it is dark, it is nice to cuddle up.
11. I do not care if you are white or grey. I know I washed you.
12. In the dark, all cats look grey.
13. If you gossip about someone, your house will burn down.
14. If you dig a ditch for someone, you yourself will fall in.
15. He knows how to lead his dog in such a way that the dog doesn't do a "doggie do" while on the leash.
16. Never leave anything till tomorrow that you can do today.

17. All people say tomorrow, tomorrow, not today.
18. Man thinks, and God guides.
19. It's raining. God is blessing us.
20. What you do not eat, the dogs and cats will.
21. All's well that ends well.
22. What Johnnie won't eat, John will.
23. What you learn when you are young, you will remember.
24. Every bean has a melody.
25. If he doesn't know what it is, he won't eat it.
26. When you go to bed, you want a partner. If you don't have a partner, you still have to go to bed.
27. Little horse, tell me a story and I will give you a crust of bread.
28. When the other girls go dancing, I will be rocking the cradle. When the other girls go to parties, I will be washing diapers.
29. Three times a day our cow eats wheat chaff out of a crooked bin.
30. Ring around the rosy, put a pot of water on the wash. Tomorrow we wash big wash and small wash.
31. Grab your own nose.
32. The apple doesn't fall far from the stem.
33. You are a dumb bunny.
34. You are good for nothing.
35. I'll go for that.
36. Don't make such a face.
37. The baker called "bake a cake", "Bake a cake", but there is no dough.
38. Well, for goodness sake.

39. The devil will eat iron as a last resort.

40. That's neither half nor whole.

41. If you don't have it in your head, you have it in your feet.

42. I have big beans in my bag.

43. Even if you are old as a cow, you will always learn more.

44. If it is small as a mouse, pick it up and take it home.

45. I am stretched to the limit like an umbrella.

46. I have an idle.

47. I fall down long and get up short.

48. The more he has, the more he wants.

49. There is a noise in the straw pile. The cat died, and the mouse was glad.

50. The cat dropped a rosy - the cat had a long tail. Tomorrow everything will be better again.

51. That's good news.

52. Whoever has nothing to do will find something to do.

53. I just remembered something.

54. Do unto me what you want others to do to you.

55. When someone goes crazy, he goes crazy in the head first.

56. You have no idea at all.

57. You are what is sitting on the telephone part (Monkey).

58. Every pot finds a lid.

59. Whoever puts his ear on the wall hears his own sins.

60. Forks, knives, and scissors are not for children.

61. When one is really hungry, a plain cake will taste good.
62. Better live life to the fullest once, rather than always so sparingly.
63. If you don't gamble, you won't win.
64. Grandmother has a long skirt and short legs.

Dennis (me), 1942

First Day of School, September, 1947

*Back from left to right: Me, Dad, Mom, my
brother Ronald; Front: my sister Linda*

Left to right: Me, Mom, Linda, Dad, 1949

Wood cutting days, 1952

My Dad, Max, 1965

The Root Cellar

Left home in 1956 in a 1936 Dodge Hearse

Berry picking with my three children

✝

Chapter Five:
My Early Teen Years

At the Age of 11

One evening, my older brother and his friends took me to a country dance. They all drank, leaving me in the hall to run around with the other kids my age. One night a man, who was approximately 35 years old, started playing with me.

Later that evening he took me out to his car, gave me a bottle of beer, then another. I thought that maybe he liked me.

One thing led to another. He took off my pants and sexually abused me. Now there was no one to talk to about this. You just didn't tell anyone about things like this. It was just another thing to add to my frustrated life.

Yes, that bothered me for many years. In my treatment in 1988, to my relief, I found that I was not responsible at that tender age. Thank you, Jesus. It was then time to deal with all the dysfunction in my life.

Now at 74 years old, I have learned about my life and have a deeper understanding of who I am in Christ. Amen.

Crying

My spirit connects with God a lot of the time. My heart breaks just as God's does because of all the sin in the world. People that reject the thought of Jesus cause me to break out in tears because I feel sad for the people that do not care.

Why I Cry

God's heart was broken and feeling pain.

In Genesis 6:5 and 6, the Lord

observed the extent of

Human wickedness on earth. He saw that

Everything they thought or

imagined was consistently and totally

Evil. So the Lord was sorry that

He had made them and put them on

Earth. It broke His heart.

I was attempting to legalize my faith

Endeavoring to design my

self-will to bear the Cross.

Afraid of getting too sentimental.

Tragedy seemed to appear. It fol-

lowed me around.

There was an ingrown sense of worthlessness.

Years were wasted for others to

understand what I know.

There was little or no sense of trust of His caring.

Studying revealed a long hard

road of religious stress.

Bent knees, wet eyes, broken

heart allows gentleness.

Walls crumble down when God steps in.

Aligned hearts with God is where

forgiveness takes place.

Grace and mercy is present when I give up.

Limiting time to talk, listen,

to obey, and to be alone.

Clouds come to carry away rain and storms.

Jesus died on the Cross in my place, crushing sin.

—DENNIS H. HOYER

Listening to Radio

One type of entertainment in the wintertime was listening to the radio, but only if conditions were favorable.

One program on the radio in the early 1950's was the National Hockey League, which then consisted of six teams. They were the Toronto Maple leafs, Montreal Canadians, Chicago Black Hawks, Detroit Red Wings, New York Rangers, and the Boston Bruins.

In it were players such a Gordie Howe, Sid Able, Ted Lindsey, Turk Broda, Ted Kennedy, Rocket Richard, Ted and Max Bentley, Gump Worsley, Terry Sawchuk, Harry Lumley, and on and on.

Other programs were *Roy Rogers, Lone Ranger and Tonto, Fibber McGee and Molly*, and *Father Knows Best*.

In the light of the mantle gas lamp, my dad shut the radio off to save the batteries so he would be able to listen to the news.

Batteries consisted of a 6-volt car battery and what was called a B battery, which was purchased at McLeod's store. When the 6-volt battery went dead, my dad would take it to the neighbors to charge it, as they had power, and it would be picked up a day or so later. Our neighbor's had electricity, but we did not. We would lie on the floor beside the wood kitchen stove, watch the fire crackle through the partial, opened draft vent of the cook stove, and listen to the radio as time allowed.

Saturday Confirmation School

I speak Blessing
- More
- Abundance
- Prosper
- Success
- Health

At about the age of thirteen, I was taking a class in church. I got strapped with a leather strap because I was not able to read or write German. When I started, school I did not know any English. (At this time in my life I was learning English. German was hardly ever spoken at home.)

Mom asked me what had happened. I told her that I had gotten strapped for not being able to read and write German. Mom never said a word. She turned and walked away from me.

Now I know, as a cop, that what had happened to Mom as a child was not dealt with.

That is family stuff that gets carried on from generation to generation. The cycle has to eventually be broken in order for the person to be freed from its grip on their life.

Trapping: Age 10 to 14

Wintertime was the time I went trapping on Saturdays. I would place a horse collar on my horse Babe with a long rope from the collar back to the front of the toboggan and back to the collar. That would give me about 25 feet behind the horse. Long reins from the horse's mouth-bit to me were made out of binder twine.

Sloughs that contained muskrat huts were visited for trapping. On the way to a muskrat house, I had a trap line set for weasels.

Some Saturdays, I would go about 6 miles to trap and visit neighbors on the way. On the toboggan, I built a box with a lid for traps and lunch. I carried a 22 rifle on my back. I was gone for the day. I loved that very much.

At nighttime, after Mom would go to bed, I would bring the dead animals into the kitchen to skin them. I would put two chairs side by side with a string tying their legs to the chair to skin them. Then the skins were put on stretchers for drying behind the kitchen stove. This was not Mom's perfect idea, but somehow she put up with it.

My dream was to get enough money together to buy a 303 used army rifle from the army surplus store in Montreal for $18.95. The ad was in the *Western Producer* paper.

Soon I figured I had enough pelts to purchase my rifle. Rabbits were worth 10¢, muskrats were $1.50 each, and weasels were $2.00 apiece. Once a month, my dad would take the team and sleigh and go eight miles to town for groceries. Sometimes he would get together with the neighbor. They would take turns going. I think Dad went when he was out of tobacco, but he would never tell Mom that reason. (Mom never wanted him to smoke because her father died of lung cancer.) Dad always got reprimanded by Mom when he got caught at this game.

So Dad took the pelts to town to the Locker Plant. They were agents for the Hudson Bay Co. and bought the furs. Then I would get a cheque later in the mail.

After a couple of months went by, I said to Mom, "I wonder where my cheque is?"

Mom said, "Dad spent it on groceries."

I eventually found other work from the neighbors to get the money to buy the gun. Welcome to the real world, 13-year-old Dennis.

Demonic Dreams

As a young teenager around 13 or 14 years of age, I experienced what I called a demonic dream. It was very clear, and at the time of writing this book I have not forgotten it.

This incident was at the front of the old mud house. A reddish brown bull was mauling me on the ground. There were no horns on the bull, but his forehead was trampling me on the ground. I was unable to get up or away. Feeling that I was near death, helpless, and full of fear, I woke up exhausted.

My interpretation was that the devil wanted me out of the way because God had a plan for me.

There was also a second strange dream of the same nature. It always took place in a large room. In that room was a large beach ball, at least 20 feet across. As I was lying on the floor, the massive ball came on top of me. As I struggled to get out from underneath the ball, I experienced suffocation from the pressure. I was unable to get out while panicking in desperation. I usually woke up yelling wildly and in a sweat. That dream went on for many years. And as the years went on, it came less frequently. God has since taken the pain and trauma of that dream away, but not the memory Amen.

A Season on the Farm

My favorite time was harvest because the thrashing machine and a crew of about eight men came for a week. I was able to miss school. My job was to watch the horse and buggy and take a washtub of food to the gang, plus coffee cakes and pies at 10 a.m. and 3 p.m. I also could help the men load and unload the sheaves to and from the hayrack.

Before these events took place, there was bindering and stooking the grain sheaves to dry in the fields before threshing. Nowadays, it is called swathing and combining.

I still have in my possession a brown 2-gallon clay coffee jug. Mom perked coffee, poured it in the jug, added cream and sugar, and put a rag around a stick of wood, which would hold fast for a trip to the field.

Every year was a routine cycle of gathering food for the family through all seasons. One must start somewhere to explain the program to ensure the food supply and/or survival of the so-called species.

In mid-January, we would fill the ice house, which was our so-called refrigerator for the summer months, with chipped ice from a nearby slough. Then a hayrack of straw was hauled on top of the ice as insulation to prevent rapid thawing in the summer.

Next came butchering one fat steer and two fairly large pigs. First was the steer. My dad, brother, and I would lead the steer from the barn to the killing area by two ropes, with me prodding it with a stick. In the killing area, there was a cross log piece up above, which was used to hang two block and tackles to hoist the steer up once he was dead so that we could butcher it.

In the early years, Dad would hit the steer with an axe on the head knocking it out. Once on the ground, Dad would cut the throat so the animal would bleed and die. Once the animal was skinned and hung up, the insides of the steer were taken out. Then it was left to hang there to cool and age for a couple of days.

As the years went by, it became my job to clobber the steer on the head, knocking it down, while my dad slit the throat. Sometimes it happened to be my pet for the last two years. Needless to say, I usually shed tears. However, that was life on the farm and emotions were never discussed. One just did what had to be done.

My brother, two years older, never enjoyed the gruesome stuff either.

For many years that was the routine. By 1970, Dad had passed away. We then had one steer left over, as the herd was sold beforehand. We needed to use the same procedure of bringing the animal to the killing station to be tied up from both sides securely by ropes. My brother stayed far to the rear. Picking up the axe, checking all circumstances to ensure all was well, I wound up, swung, and stuck the steer hard between the eyes. Down it fell to the ground, shivering and convulsing. I, as usual, knew the job was done. I will never, ever forget the next step as long as I live.

There was a moment of tense silence, and I felt frozen with emotion. I stared at the butcher knife sticking out of the snow on the ground. The knife didn't move; there was no one else around. I had a stark, paralyzing moment of realization. With tears in my eyes, I became aware that I was next in line to get the job done. Dad was not there. He was gone. No one was there to help. Emptiness and abandonment jarred my soul as never before.

My legs felt frozen to my body. It seemed I was not able to move. Every muscle in my body creaked with fear. I was about to perform the most ugly and gruesome task of my life.

Finally, the knife was brought to the convulsing, dying animal. I cut the throat to let the gushing, thick blood flow onto the ground and snow. I watched the animal slowly stop moving and dying.

What I now believe is that at 30 years of age God spoke to me. "Your dad is gone, never to come back. You are it. You are the next generation. It is time to grow up and take responsibility." My guts girded up. The tears stopped. I had to begin growing up now. I had to take charge and get the job done.

As evening grew into darkness, from a cold seat in the outdoor toilet, I sat and watched the still carcass hanging dead, butchered in the trees. I felt that there were ghosts going to come and get me – eerie to say the least. I didn't have anyone to share all my emotions with.

Next came the butchering of two pigs. This was a slightly different procedure. Pigs were shot in the head, the blood was drained, and there was a big fire built to heat approximately 50 gallons of scalding hot water. Once the dead pig was lying in a scalding tub, the hot water was poured over the carcass. Then the hair was scraped off of the bodies. Shortly after the bodies were cleaned, they were hung up to cool off for a few days.

The next step was to cut up the three animals in certain stages. Steak, sausage, bacon, pressma (liver sausage), head cheese, and on and on. There was lots of canning in sealers for the root cellar shelves.

Hams and bacon were put into barrels of brine to cure. Sausage, bacon, and ham were all hung in the smoke house in the porch of the ice house. Heavy smoke from the willow trees sealed the meat. It would hang there all summer and more until used. That meat never spoiled or the flies never went near the food.

One time as a kid, the kitchen table was completely full of all kinds of meat, sealers, tubs, and the sausage machine. It was lunchtime. Mom gave me a plate of food and said, "Sit down and eat." While walking around the table looking for a spot to place my plate, I found one. Yes, between the two pigs' heads that were cut off from their bodies at the shoulders. The snouts were still on the heads. I stared into their dead eyes during my meal. Yes, no complaining. Food was home cooked and good.

After harvest, the next step was to go into the bush to cut down trees, plus gather the fallen ones. Anywhere from 30 to 60 sleigh loads were brought home. Then on Saturdays, a crew of neighbors would help one another to cut wood and pile it up high for the year.

Now one of the last remaining tasks was to cut blocks of ice and drag them to the back of the house. Ice would be broken up during the winter. The chips were placed in a reservoir of a cook stove where it would melt for household use. There was also a large barrel there that was used to thaw ice for bathing.

I remember one October, my birthday month, we picked potatoes, bagged them, and loaded them onto a flat horse-drawn wagon. At seven p.m., it was dark as we made our way to the root cellar. We stopped in front of the house for supper. Mom had a birthday cake for me. We ate quickly, went to unload the 30 bags of potatoes, then went to bed. That is the only time I remember ever celebrating my birthday.

Tumbleweed

Christine, you are not a tumbleweed

Dearly hanging on a fence to survive

Storms are not forcing you to spread love

You are free through Christ to be alive

Dream as a child belly laughing in green grass
Lofty mountains peaks beckoning
where alpine flowers grow
Do not allow a holy morning to turn to nothing
Dew dropped roses glimmer for sun to show

Your life is moon-covered with sparkling stars
While gazing over landscapes
smelling spring wet earth
Paint a picture of Jesus in the confused world
You are equipped for a challenge from birth

Preparing to hear the sounds of a lost soul
Your caring tentative ear will be aware of pain
Tears rejoicing praise abounding for angels above
Songs of glory will rise up for your gain

You are a vessel upon a skyline of a sea
Enduring high waves roaring
against a rocky shore
Vast depth of your soul allows seeing beyond,

Your heartbeat is assurance

that discord is no more

Nothing is as strong as gentleness

Nothing is as gentle as real strength

—DENNIS H. HOYER

Leaving Home at 16 – 1956

From the age of 14, some opportunities arose for me to make a bit of money. Odd jobs seemed to turn up, such as driving neighbors' tractors in the summertime for field work, blacksmith work, driving tractor on a binder at harvest time, sweeping granaries out, plus other jobs. I got enough money to raise a couple of pigs, plus I raised pumpkins.

As I am writing this book, I am remembering thoughts on how I survived my childhood. There were three neighbors. As I think about who would know of the abuse I was suffering, they would likely have put two and two together. They were the ones who always helped me in whatever way they could without my parents knowing what was going on.

One neighbor lived one mile to the west, another one lived a half mile southwest. Another one, was about five miles to the west. They were on my trap line, and they would always talk to me. They would let me trap on their land and feed me on the way through.

I turned sixteen in October 1956. Then in the springtime of 1957, I failed grade nine. At that point, I decided to leave home. I quit school about April or May because I got 10% on a test for neatness…because there was nothing on it. A total blank!!!

Somehow on a trip to town an opportunity arose from a man who owned a construction company. He needed someone to help him in his shop to get ready to build roads in the summer. I very clearly remember the day. My brother worked at a funeral home and sold me a 1936 Dodge Black hearse for 100 dollars. I had $300 in my pocket that I had scared up from selling eight piglets. I had one change of clothes.

From that day on to this day, I have never been out of work.

On my first job, I eventually got to operate road construction equipment, but I earned very little money. A year later, I bought a 1950 Pontiac car. I borrowed the money ($300) from the local grain buyer. I paid him back in four months.

One summer I worked at a construction camp out in no man's land. Most of the guys would leave Saturday at noon for who knows where. They would be back at work the next Monday morning. But I never had money for gas, friends, or anywhere to go.

The sleeping bunk trailer was there, open with a bed for me to sleep in. The cookhouse was locked up so there was no food. I remember eating a moldy crust of bread that I found under the men's beds. I became very sick the next Monday, but I went to work and never said a word to anyone because of shame.

As the winter freeze-up came around in late fall, I would find a dairy farm to milk cows and shovel manure for the winter, so I would have free room and board. Eventually, I got to drive a milk truck, which went to the dairy farmers and took their milk to the city.

Later I got a truck driving job in the city, plus numerous other jobs such as selling life insurance. I was never successful, as I am not a salesman. I worked for the Goodyear Tire Company and the city transit. In 1963, I got married. One son was born in 1966, and one son was born in 1968. My daughter came along in 1973.

✝

Chapter Six:
My Adult Years

Snake in My Face

Age 17 this experience took place in my car. My buddy and I were in Regina, and we had purchased a gallon of red wine. We gulped down a good dose of wine in the parking lot. That produced a good jag on. We then started to drive north out of town. My car was a 1950 Pontiac Torpedo car. The exhaust pipe was broken off at the manifold, which caused a deafening sound while travelling at 90 mph and through red lights. We almost ran over a pedestrian in the middle of the street on the way to a small town dance approximately 60 miles away.

We often drove many miles, drinking wine out of a glass jug on the shoulder. We both seemed to be going blind. Through the ditch, into a farmer's field...that's where the car stalled. That is also where we both passed out. At approximately 11 a.m. on a

Sunday morning, I woke up. There was a blinding hot sun, the windows shut, and we were almost suffocating. I woke up. My buddy was passed out in the driver's seat where he had fallen asleep. I had fallen against him.

My stomach wanted to toss its cookies, plus I had a splitting headache. I needed to get some air. That car had vent windows that could be opened up to allow air to come into the car. The vent windows were approximately 10″ high and were V-shaped. They were 6 inches wide at the base.

While coming to my senses, I observed a boa constrictor head jammed in that window taking up all the space of the V-shaped window. I was staring into the ugly face of the snake, which was terrible enough. The snake had two black, shiny, firm split tongues that were flashing about an inch from my face. That was my first experience with the DTs, as they call it. I tell you that was not a nice place or situation to be in. I continued to drink until April 25, 1982. I have not had a drink since then.

Approximately five years ago, in 2009, I was assisting a friend on his ranch with harvesting. I was repairing a hay silo feeder chain. My friend was lifting the chain assembly up with a tractor front-end loader. The chain slipped off, and 2000 pounds of steel crashed and pined me against the wall, breaking my leg. The ambulance took me to Medicine Hat Hospital where the doctors put a steel pin in my lower leg.

Strong medications were prescribed. Wow, the medications were so strong, they put me to sleep.

While sleeping, I had a nightmare in which I was lying in a rail boxcar, but the boards were missing and the wild, frigid wind was blowing over me.

Mom and I Discussing My Dad's Death

After Dad passed away in 1970, I went out to get Mom to do some business in Regina. On the way home, Mom out and told me that after reading Dad's will she was very angry because my dad had left his estate to us children so that we would look after mom. The rest of the money was split up three ways between us three children.

Dig Deeper

He wants me to live and show His purpose.

Trees grounded in rocks learn to talk to the sky.

Tears are shed, equipping me

for nourishing vigor.

My shadows of life are created by His sunlight.

His words soak my soul with sustaining life

Tears of God surround my grateful heart.

My tears are for those who have no trust in Him.

From earth, Christ promises my

story will be recorded.

The earth is a garden. The Lord is the gardener.

God planted in my soul an affectionate seed.

Growing on this earth through

birth pains were grim.

My decaying body will soon

pass over these trials.

A new glorified body will be

in heaven for eternity.

Desiring to know my loving great almighty God.

I want to go home and spend time with Him.

This is my story. This is my song.

—DENNIS H. HOYER

Dreams of Being in Love

Searching for a rainbow on grassy hills

Brilliant colored hues "settle

on my heart" as it fills

My Lord inspires my essence / with

 solace prayer

Bouquets of charm / show how much I care

Butterflies flutter towards my windowsill

Becoming heavenly angels seeking God's will

Sun warming emerald / transform

landscape green

Pale moon not casting

shadows / where I have been

Tear drops shedding / are pennies turning gold

Risking through delusions of

truth / before getting old

Past heartaches are softening / through grace

Being inspired / by the rosy

prudent look on your face

Roads of loneliness / directed for peaceful joy

Maturity uncovering sudden

change / with some coy

Smoldering embers spawn

flames / not to be put out

Upfront Christian values

declare / what you are about

Aroused by the fact / I am forgiven / he told

Eternally grateful / Jesus

accepted me / for his fold

Suffered sinless / nothing for

himself / only for me

Death on the Cross he rose for my sins to be free

Love is simple / you simply are love

Without demands or expectations / love just is

The voice of love is calling / out to you

Love is the voice of God / whispering

to you / from within

—DENNIS H. HOYER

My Visions and Dreams

I still have dreams of adventure in my life. They are:
- Gold panning in British Columbia
- Watching salmon runs
- Watching bald eagles migrate
- Visiting the *U.S. Missouri* battleship in Hawaii
- Taking a ride on a Lancaster bomber in Ottawa
- Playing guitar and singing country gospel

My hobbies are woodworking, restoring antique tractors, and grand kids (7).

I have only one mission at my age and that is to lead people to Christ.

Returning to School

In 1967, while being employed by the city of Regina as a transit driver, I decided to go back to school. I had failed grade 9 at the farm school. My intention was to get my grade 12 and become a conservation officer. I took many vocational classes, but at the end of the year, I flunked English and History. So there I was.

The certificate from Balfour Technical gave me a vocational grade ten. I worked at a steel plant for a year and applied at the police service. I worked nights, shaking doors on a beat in Regina. It was a good job. I kept my mouth shut and enjoyed my secure job.

Five years later, I got my grade 12 through night classes and correspondence at the age of 32. Amen.

I started working with the Regina Police in 1969, and retired in 1994 with a survivable pension.

Kim's Sickness

My son Kim was born in 1968. There were a few crises that happened in his life, and I will list them as I remember them. He was born on September 1, and he came home at the end of February 1969, weighing 10 lbs. He was born with a bowel dysfunction. Kim had many surgeries by doctors in Regina and Winnipeg, and many times it was very clear to me that he was going to die.

It was during my final exams when I first went back to school that my one-year-old son became ill with infection. I went to school in the daytime and stayed in the hospital with my son at night to hold his tube. That way he could hold his favorite bear called Titter.

Age 3, he fell out of the back window of my station wagon while it was up on a ramp getting an oil change. He fell on his head, smashing it two-thirds of the way around. The cracks on the x-ray looked like a smashed egg. He was unconscious for 3 days. Later he fell down a flight of stairs, banging his head. He was not hospitalized for this.

Then he fell out of the car on the #1 highway in Banff, Alberta. I noticed him in the review-mirror lying on the highway. He was not hospitalized that time either. Then when Kim was at school, he fell on the ice on the playground. This time he was unconscious and was hospitalized for a few days.

Throughout the 1960's, there were a few times when I did not have a job. The government at that time had introduced deterrent fees. I cannot remember the dollar amount per day in the hospital. As well, the Saskatchewan government would not pay the fee for the operation in Winnipeg because they felt that the procedure could have been done in Saskatchewan.

While my son was in the Winnipeg hospital, a doctor somehow came across my son's bowel problem. The doctor was a heart surgeon. He had taken schooling in regards to my son's problem and had become an expert in that area as well. Thus, he decided to take on the challenge and do Kim's surgery.

Months after my son's recovery, I went to this doctor and met with him in his office. My bill from this doctor was $10,000. That was a lot of money in those days. My story was only the truth. I was out of work with no savings. However, my message was that I was willing to work out some type of payment structure to pay off the bill.

This doctor just calmly looked at me and stated, "Dennis, I forgive that bill. You do not have to pay for it."

On a side note, an experience while sitting with my son in the hospital: About 4:00 a.m. in the morning, a doctor was walking in the hallway carrying something. It was sponge board with a 10-inch-long baby taped on it.

Afterwards, the doctor told me the following: Many years ago, the old doctors would see something like this. They would lay the baby aside for a few minutes while tidying up a few tools. The doctor would casually go back to the baby, he would see that the baby had died, and he would say something like, "Oops, oh well." The baby had passed away. There would be war over that today because it would not be accepted.

That was forty years ago. Now as a Christian, I know that at the time of conception this baby was a human being. That baby is now in heaven.

Ripping out Nicole's Bedroom Wall

One day in about 1975, a wild, furious screaming match between my wife and myself broke out in front of the three children at home. I lost complete control of the situation and was in full rage mode at the height of the argument.

I went into my daughter's bedroom, fists clenched, screaming at the top of my voice, and started to punch the wall with my bare fists. I was pounding, ripping, tearing, and grabbing pieces of gyprock with my trembling hands. My body was numb. I felt no pain or reasoning.

A section of the wall approximately 5 feet by 6 feet was ripped out bare-handed. While tearing out nails and pieces of whatever, my hands and arms were deeply cut, and I started bleeding from the open wounds.

After that demonstration of being a total maniac in operation, I went in to the kitchen where my three kids were standing against the stove with wide teary eyes. They were totally immersed in fear for their lives. My wife was screaming at me words I do not recall.

Like a raging idiot, with arms flailing and splashing blood on the wall, I laid the law down to the family. Pointing fingers I stated I was the boss of this family from now on. I would be in charge, and everyone had to do as I said. Talk about fear, emptiness, remorse, helpless, and nowhere to turn.

Writing this book, looking back now, I know my life was a tragedy.

Now I am aware that God is driven with a deep compassion for souls.

When our hearts and minds align with God, we are forgiven.

Tears sustain us with despair. There is hope.

When my walls came down, God came in.

Tears will become my food, and they will equip me.

"In the broken heart of God, He felt my pain."
Genesis 6:5, 6

Joe Barnes

In about 1950, in a nearby town, lived a man who I will call Joe Barns.

My family came to town a couple of times in the summer for an outing. A few other town kids and I would gather to show each other how smart we had become by smoking, getting dizzy, and swearing. Sometimes there were a few beers.

There was a local man who seemed to be everywhere. He was slightly mentally challenged. Most of the immature kids seemed to get a charge by poking fun at him. That was some of our entertainment, making the others get a laugh from it.

Twenty-five years later while painting a lady's house, I observed a man sitting in the shade, crying beside the house next door. After sometime I remembered that this was the man Joe Barnes.

Coming down the ladder, I walked over to Joe to talk to him, as he appeared to be somewhat distressed.

A few minutes passed. I asked him if he had summoned me. He replied, "Yes." Well, my mind started to race. I observed his quivering chin lowered on his chest. He was staring at his feet, while he weaved from side to side, holding his face, and wiping tears from his cheeks.

I asked, "Why are you feeling so terrible, and can I be of any help to you?"

After a few moments, sniffing back the tears, Joe shared his dilemma.

Joe made this statement: "You know, Dennis. I walk all night to every house. There are approximately 100 of them. I go under their bedroom window and say a prayer for those inside. When the sun comes up in the morning, those people get up and see me walking down the streets. As they come out of their houses they laugh at me."

Wow that set me back for a few weeks.

I have a saying I use a lot and this applied then: "I feel so low I could walk under a snake with a high hat on."

Cuba Holiday

In 1978, during my drinking years, my wife and I and our three children – aged 12, 10, and 5 – went to Cuba for a ten-day holiday. We went at Easter time because of the school break. Another couple, that was a bit older than us, came along. They had no children with them.

On my off days during the previous summer, I had moonlighted as a housepainter for the extra money to go on that holiday. We stayed on a resort just off the beach in stone-walled huts among the trees. Each family had their own hut for the 10 days.

In those days in Cuba, the military was in charge. Basically, we were restricted to a certain area and not able to go and do as we pleased.

We went on a tour bus to the sugar cane fields plus on a countryside trip. On about the eighth day, we went on a trip to another island approximately 25 miles off of the main land. There we were given an American-style barbeque supper. It was first class in every respect. We found out later that the reason it was so far away was that, being a communist country, they did not want the local people to see such luxury.

Being where I was emotionally, concerning my wife, I do not remember sleeping with her because of the dysfunction and fighting. Many nights were spent sleeping on the beach by the ocean.

Staring into the heavens, creation's store, I became aware that God had spoken the word and all galaxies were placed there by name. When God held the whole earth in his hands, even before hanging it in the space in the universe, He said, "Dennis I love you. I will never forsake you or leave you. You are special and I will take care of you. I have a plan for your life."

One night, while stargazing I observed the Big Dipper. It was in the exact same place as it appears in the sky at home, three thousand miles away. I thought, 'My, Dennis, you just are not as great as you think you are. I am smaller than a kernel of sand on a beach beside an ocean. Not even a speck, but I still have a purpose.'

Now that I am aware that Jesus died on the Cross for all my pain, sickness, disease, and suffering. He understands what each one of us is going through.

Many years later, when I was at a Bible Study, my pastor covered the topic of eternity and what it means.

Eternity is forever, non-ending peace, love, and joy. With Jesus, there is no pain or suffering, no earthly thoughts. We will live in a new heavenly body.

Eternity is when a robin takes one grain of sand in its beak, then flies all the way to the moon and deposits it there. Then it comes back to earth for another grain of sand. The robin repeats the same scenario over and over, from the earth to the moon. When that robin completes that process millions of times or until the whole earth is gone, that is when eternity begins.

Praise Jesus. Amen.

Chapter Seven:
Seven near-death Experiences

These seven stories are reminders of how God kept me during the time of my life when I was floundering, not sure of who I was and where I belonged in life. These were stepping stones in my journey to bring me to where I am today. Number seven is the number of completion in the Bible which indicates that it will not ever happen again. And that is comforting.

1. Driving Home After a Date - 1962

At approximately 2:00 a.m. one summer night, I was driving home on a country road from a date. I had a few beers in my belly.

The car was a 1949 Chevy two-door sedan, six cylinder, torpedo backed, and pink and blue in color.

My trip would have been thirty-five miles in distance on a grid road. This was 6 or 7 miles from my hometown where I was to be at work at 7 a.m.

As I remember the incident, I was falling asleep, head bobbing, while feeling a sleepiness coming over me. Next thing, I felt my car swaying back and forth. Losing control and hitting the right soft shoulder of the road, I heard the car skidding sideways. Then before I knew it, the car was rolling and rolling – four times in all. As it continued to roll, I hit the roof with a heavy thump that jarred my head and neck, just as the car flipped onto the roof. It knocked me unconscious. I woke up around 6 a.m. with the sun shining.

I began to retrace the steps of what had happened. I had started out, travelling northbound. I had no idea how fast I had been going, but my car had rolled four times in the ditch.

When I awoke, there was a foot of loose earth that had completely covered me from head to toe. I shrugged my head, shaking off the dirt, and tried to get my bearings. In daylight, I noticed the following: My car had slid sideways for some distance, with the passenger door wide open. This is the miracle that is hard to explain.

While unconscious from the blow on the back of my head, I was thrown out of the car through the passenger side door, and landed on a rock pile, covered with dirt. At the same time, the whole car filled up with dirt. The car came to a stop against a fence gatepost. The passenger side door was open beside the post. I was on the other side of the post. The post was in between me and the car. I was on my stomach, wrapped around the post, completely covered with dirt. I will never figure out how I got from the driver's seat and out through the passenger door. The car landed upside down, also completely filled with dirt.

When I got up, I shook of the dirt. There was not a scratch on my body. I then hitchhiked to town and made it to work on time. Thank you Jesus. Amen.

2. Police Car – 1972

My marriage was very stormy. We went for help 22 times in 23 years. There just seemed to always be something to argue about. My favorite saying was "like mixing oil and water".

One afternoon on a cold, stormy winter day, a disagreement took place before I left for work. I had made my lunch and put it in a tin lunch box. The disagreement was escalating as I was going out the door. Out on the driveway, I remembered I had not taken my lunch. Turning towards the house, my wife opened the door and threw the lunch pail at me. It struck and cut my face and twisted my glasses. There was blood running down my face onto my uniform. What were the guys at the station going to say about this? Grabbing handfuls of snow, I placed it over my face to stop the oozing blood and attempted to clean the stains off of my uniform. I then straightened out my glasses and placed them back on my face.

I got to work just in time for detailing in the parade room. While sitting at the very back, my face must have been a bit pale in color. The sergeant said to the guys, "What is wrong with Bunker?" (My nickname). Twenty-five guys all turned around to look at me. They said, "He is okay. He probably is not getting any tail at home." They laughed and got on with business.

Before this incident took place, my plan had been to get in my police car, book out at the hospital, and get medical attention as if I were on an investigation. But when I got in my police car, my mind went blank.

I somehow got to the Exhibition grounds and parked the car bumper against a totem pole in the parking lot. A winter blizzard was blowing snow across the pavement. There was absolutely no thought about anything or anybody.

I reached on my right side and pulled out my police revolver. (Note: As I am writing this story, I can feel the cold steel in my mouth and taste and smell the gun powder.) My index finger was starting to squeeze the trigger.

This is the only time throughout my life that I heard the deep, loud, thunderous, audible voice of God speaking to me. He (God) said, "Dennis, put it away. I will look after you." I put the gun away and He did. Thank you Jesus. Amen.

As I came back to reality, I realized that attempted suicide was a criminal offence and because of that I could lose my job. I carried that guilt into the Treatment Centre in Mandan, North Dakota in 1988 and dealt with it there.

Tensions were building to an extreme tempo in the fall of 1988 in our home. Lying on the couch, I was not able to comprehend my thoughts at that time. My time was spent lying on the chesterfield in the living room listening to Billy Graham, Tennessee Ernie Ford, and Johnny Cash for some relief.

Arguments were very frequent, and the battles were skyrocketing with no resolution. On my day off in about mid-November, I was unable to go into the house as my back was under so much tension. After a night on the chesterfield, I managed to get up and was able to get into my truck. I had no plans except to just get off the yard. After one hour, I found myself setting at a Franciscan retreat house looking out the large windows.

Some time had passed when a priest walked by and asked, "What is it with you young man?" He invited me into the office. Sitting across from me at his desk, the priest just looked at me. I told about ten minutes of my story and what had been happening in my life.

The priest picked up his cane and with a hard jolt jammed it in my forehead with a thud. The priest told me to go and see a lawyer and get out of the marriage.

Now what? I had never, ever thought of divorce or leaving. So upon leaving, I went and saw a lawyer to see what my options were.

3. Before Mandan

Going home, I attempted to come to some resolutions, but I realized that none were coming my way.

A few weeks later, on December 20, 1988, there was a rumble in the house. I went from room to room, attempting to get some reprieve from all that had been taking place. On December 23, it all came to a head. I finally crawled into a large closet and pulled two feet of clothes to each side of my head to stop the noise. I wanted the fighting to stop. I was getting serious about doing something or causing harm that I would regret. God gave me a vision. I looked towards the entrance door of the house. My vision was that two of my police buddies would come and lock me up.

I then made a concerted decision right there and then. The decision was I wanted to be a father to my three children. I did not want to be a father who was in jail or in an insane asylum or dead –as I was ready to kill myself. I got up, locked myself in the bathroom until the fighting subsided, and called for help. I did not know where my children were.

Then on Christmas Eve, I turned myself in to a help centre. My comrades came and took me down to Mandan, North Dakota. They dropped me off, and I spent 28 days there.

First they took me to a room with an examination table. I was stripped naked, deloused, and my belongings were taken from me. I was a total basket case. Listening to Christmas carols in the background, an old doctor told me, "Dennis, this place will look after and take care of you. As you are at the right age to be helped, we will help you make wise decisions for your future." Then the rubber glove came on. He said, "Bend over." (Merry Christmas, Dennis.) After 10 days I had a talk with God. He asked me, "What do you want?" I said, "I want my children and my marriage.

But I do not know how to do it. I know I need your help." I never went home.

I owe my life to the founders of Alcohol Anonymous. There is hope!!

4. Apartment Building near Miss – 1989

In the springtime of 1989 I was in divorce proceedings and living in total uncertainty of the future in all facets of my life. I was slowing stepping in to some depression, as my life was not happening as I had planned.

I had an old 1969 Ford square box van. On a dark evening, my mind took off in a dark downturn once more. Just to the east of me, at a dead end street, were a row of apartment blocks. The apartments were about 10 to 12 blocks away.

Getting the old van in high gear, at about 60 mph, I was accelerating madly towards the face of the brick apartment building.

The van flew over the sidewalk, bouncing violently across the lawn. This was the second place where God intervened once again. I said to myself, "I am living in hell, and I am going to hell."

A few years previous, a pastor had told me that Satan has no power over me. I said, "Be gone Satan, you have no power over me." With a hard right, my hands cramping on the steering wheel, I missed the building by no more than six inches. That was the last time I ever had those suicidal thoughts. Thank you, Jesus. He will never, ever leave me nor forsake me. Amen.

5. Motorcycle in B.C.

In 1989, my son and I decided to go to British Columbia to visit an uncle and aunt of mine on our motorcycles.

It was a beautiful October day as we proceeded west. As we approached the mountains, we met up with a snowstorm. Eventually, we got to Merritt B.C. We rented a motel room. There we ran the bathtub full of hot water, both taking turns for a few minutes at a time to thaw out. The next morning, we got a good start. We arrived at the hill leading into Salmon Arm, B.C. We stopped to rest and get a bite to eat. We filled our pockets up with nice fresh fruit and took off down a beautiful hill to the flats of the highway.

My son was wearing a yellow rain suit and was in the lead. I was cruising in the beautiful sun-filled day with no worries, just enjoying my fresh fruit.

Then, for a minute, I did not see my son's yellow jacket down ahead of me on the road. Looking up, there was a semi-trailer truck heading my direction on my side of the road facing me. He started passing a line of traffic and could not get back in on his side as he was coming down the other side of the mountain. A split second passed. "Oh my God, there are no shoulders on these highways through the mountains." Peering down to the road on the right side, I saw a 2-foot shoulder ledge. I jerked the bike to the right as much as I could. That truck went on coming, passing the line of cars towards me. The wheels of the truck touched my leg. Another inch and I would not have been here writing this story. Amen.

6. Moose Hunting

One of my pastimes was hunting. This incident happened about the year 2000, while I was moose hunting in the area of Hudson Bay, Saskatchewan. After eight years of moose hunting in this area, I had ever seen only one moose cross the trail in the bush.

This particular trip of four days was exciting because I would get a hotel room in a small town nearby where I was hunting. My half-ton was not a 4 by 4 and was almost useless, however I had a trailer and an old skidoo to help me out.

After enjoying an open fire dinner, which is really living in my books, I unloaded the skidoo, packed a bit of lunch, took my trusty .30-06, and headed out for an evening hunt with about one hour of daylight left.

There are many trails to explore in God's Paradise in the northern forests, and it also gets very dark early in the day. I came up to quite a large lake, which in my opinion was a perfect location for a moose hunt. It was a perfect evening with loose snow to travel on for a beautiful sightseeing tour. I passed through a small bay with a patch of bull rushes. Pulling up to where the weeds were, my skidoo broke through the ice. With only one foot of the ski out on the ice, three-quarters of the machine was in the water. I fell into the icy water, and my skidoo boots and skidoo seat quickly filled up with ice water. I was sinking.

What now? Something told me to stop and think this through. As I was hanging onto the back end of the machine, assessing the situation, I thought, 'If I pull too hard on the skidoo, it will drop in to the water and then that would be the end.' Bobbing in the water, my eyes locked onto a bull rush plant sticking through the ice in front of the sled.

Slowly I got myself moving up and down in the water, hoping to get high enough to grab the plant right so it did not break off. As God would have it, I gently eased myself with the right hand on the skidoo. Like a walrus, I slid on top of the ice only to roll away from the water hole. Thank you, Jesus.

Now there was a faint glimmer of daylight left, so draining out the bulk of the water out of my boots and clothing, I walked to shore.

When I got to where I had come in, I saw my tracks in the snow. This was another stroke of luck from above. Being aware that the truck was about a mile away, in the cold pitch-blackness of night, I felt the skidoo tracks in the snow and touching the trees, I was able walk to the truck. Then unhooking the trailer, I drove to the shore where the sled was. Being in the possession of a 100-foot rope, I fastened the rope to the rear of the truck and walked to the dreaded water hole that had the skidoo sticking out of it. Rolling towards the machine, I tied the rope to a ski, and then pulled myself on the rope back towards the truck. My feet were frozen, but once in the truck, I took my boots off and warmed my feet by the truck heater while pulling the skidoo to where the trailer was. I winched it onto the trailer and drove to the hotel.

At 4:00 a.m., I was cold, wet, hungry, and tired. I had a can of beans and some pop and went to bed. I fell asleep, thanking God I was okay. Amen.

7. Vulcan, Alberta

In 2002, I bought a small 600-square-foot mobile home in Vulcan, Alberta. One side of the trailer was a lean-to with a heated garage. This was a place for me to put my woodworking shop, with a place at the back to use as a single car garage.

At a church I attended on a regular basis, I had met lots of nice people.

One farmer, who I had gotten to know after meeting him at church, had a few old grain bins at his place. With excitement I observed that the bins were built in the 1920's to the 1930's. The boards were old and grey. That barn wood was excellent for all kinds of furniture to sell at the local flea market.

One day, I was out in the field, removing boards from the sides of the grain bins, one board at a time. I was working across the building from the bottom up until all four sides were clear of siding boards. My intentions were to make the building fall to the ground in a designed direction.

The striped bin was beside a thin-strand barbed fence for cattle. There was room to only walk sideways between the building and a four-strand fence. The wires were as tight as guitar strings. I was half way to the other side when there was tremendous crack.

The building had started to topple in the opposite way from what I had planned.

Immediately I thought, 'the building is going down, and there is nowhere for me to go.'

I had to make a split-second decision. I remembered the tight fence wire and that there would be no give in that wire fence. I had to get out of the way of the falling building. In shear fright, I leaned against the fence with all my might. Three inches allowed me the space to avoid the crashing building.

My right shoulder, arm, and legs were grazed by the falling building before it hit the ground. Again, the amazing power of a supernatural hand of God had spared my life once more.

This is the last of the seven times God intervened to spare my life. He has a plan for me.

Throughout my life I have learned that the number 7 is a number of completion. It is so reassuring that the curses are now behind me. Thank you Jesus. Amen.

Chapter Eight:
New Hope

Treatment Centre in Regina - 1983

At one point in 1983, I was starting to change for a few months. My heart wanted a change. While I was in a Treatment Centre in Regina, attempting to save my marriage, I spent 28 days taking a look at myself.

On November 27, 1983, I went for a walk at 10:00 p.m. in Victoria Park. It was a snowy winter night. Walking past a war memorial, looking up at the flood-lights through the drifting snow, I called out loud, "Jesus, come into my life." At that moment, I hit the ground like a chicken with its head cut off. I was fluttering in two feet of snow amongst the fir trees. I had no idea what happened after that. I woke up the next morning at the Treatment Centre.

February 12, 1984, while at a church, I went to the altar for prayer. A minute later I received the baptism of the Holy Spirit with the gift of speaking in tongues. (While on a mission trip in Mexico in January 2010, I was baptized by water submersion. What a cleansing experience.)

Throughout the above experience, I still had hardness living in my heart. I was trying to live the true life of Christ, but honestly never walked the walk, which led to me running into much trouble. For example, being in a casino, gambling at 4 a.m. in the morning. I was down $500. Things were becoming desperate, but God jolted a memory of something I had heard many years ago.

Someone once said, "If you knew that you would die at this very moment would you be proud of what you were doing? What would Jesus say to you at the pearly gates?" I thought about it for a moment. Guess what I did next? I checked my pulse and my breathing capacity and decided that I was not going to die right then. I wanted to retrieve my lost money and then gamble some more. Now really, is that not truly spitting in God's face? I was continuing in the same destructive way of living and expecting different results. What was I thinking?

One thing after another led me to places that I had no idea about how I got there.

In 2001, I moved to Calgary and worked at some construction while also looking after an apartment. I had never had a cent to my name. Yes, I had my pension, but that was not enough.

Thankfully, my sons helped me out some. Thank you Jesus. Amen.

Moving to Calgary

I made a call to a recommended realtor to see if there was a possibility I would be able to borrow some money to purchase a trailer to live in. The realtor called back within one hour stating that because I have never ever missed any type of payment and had an excellent track record, he would be able to help me. Then he asked me how much money I needed. I bought a trailer with a workshop in Vulcan, Alberta. There I lived for two years. I gathered scrap wood from construction sites in Calgary. Plus I got to know some farmers who would give away old granaries for barn wood. I would build rustic furniture and then sell it at flea markets to survive.

I lived there for two years, then sold the trailer making $2000 on it. That gave me a down payment. I purchased a house in Lethbridge, but it was way over my head financially. After one year, I sold it and made a good profit on it as the market was hot at that time in Alberta. I then purchased acreage in Wildwood, Alberta. After moving to Wildwood, I was to go for testing for colon cancer. Now what? I put my place up for sale. In those days, one was able to make a fair dollar. I got on the computer, and for days I searched for a place to live on my income.

British Columbia, Alberta, and Saskatchewan. Where should I go? Maple Creek seemed to fit the bill. I have now been here for nine years. Hey, and guess what? I have no cancer. Praise Jesus. Amen.

Lancaster Bomber Pilot's Flight Plan – 2004

During my adult years I was enamored with the two world wars, the people, the planes, the battles, etc. So when I met this pilot it was truly a dream come true to visit with him and hear his stories.

On Christmas Eve in 2004, I decided to go and do visitation at the hospital. When I arrived, I went to the main office requesting the okay to come and work the halls and visit the patients. After the R.C.M.P. check, I was cleared to spend the night, keeping patients company to get over some of their loneliness.

Late in the night, an older gentleman called to me out of his dark room. He asked me to come and sit beside him if that would be all right. He said that he was on a bombing run and that he was in charge and I should not worry. He said that he would take us in and get us out safely.

After some time of talking, I became aware that he had been a Lancaster bomber pilot in WWII. At that time, I was a World War II history buff, especially interested in Lancaster bombers.

Although the man was suffering from Alzheimer's, his wartime stories were extremely interesting. For that he had a good memory of that time and place in his life.

When our visit came to a close, he gave me the following mission log on one of his flights over Germany. Bombing raids. Was I excited or what!!!

The following is the log in the exact format that I received from him.

23/24 FEB. 1945   PFORZHEIM:

367 LANCASTERS and 13 MOSQUITOES
OF 1, 6 and 8 GROUPS

1 FILM UNIT LANCASTER

10 LANCASTERS LOST and 2 MORE
CRASHED IN FRANCE.

FIRST and ONLY AREA-BOMBING
RAID OF WAR ON THIS TARGET.

VERY ACCURATE MARKING and
BOMBING FROM ONLY 8,000 FT.

1825 TONS OF BOMBS DROPPED IN 22 MINUTES.

AREA OF 3 KM BY 1 ½ KM COMPLETELY
ENGULFED BY FIRE

CAUSING DEATHS OF 17, 6000 PEOPLE.

THIRD HEAVIEST DEATH TOLL IN
GERMANY DURING WAR.
FOLLOWING HAMBURG and DRESDEN.
83% OF TOWN'S BUILT UP AREA
DESTROYED (GREATEST PROPORTION
IN ONE RAID DURING WAR)

BOMBER COMMAND'S LAST VICTORIA
CROSS OF WAR WON ON THIS RAID

CPTN. EDWIN SWALES D.F.C., A SOUTH
AFRICAN MASTER BOMBER

WITH 582 SON, HIS LANCASTER WAS
DAMAGED BY ENEMY FIGHTERS

OVER TARGET. HE WAS KILLED IN THE CRASH
AFTER ORDERING CREW TO BALE OUT.

625 SON FORMED IN 1 GROUP WITH
LANCASTERS 1/10/43 AT KELSTERN (LINCS)

UNTIL NEARLY END OF WAR and THEN FLEW 5
RAIDS FROM SCAMPTON (LINCS) IN APRIL '45.

FLEW 3,385 SORTIES   LOST 66 A/C. (1.9%)

191 BOMBING RAIDS and 2 MINELAYING RAIDS

8 LANCASTERS WERE DESTROYED IN CRASHES.

16 M   ALAN ROFF.

History in Poetry

Responding to a divine calling of conjugation
Seed with egg united for new creation
Soul of God now will be shielded
by flesh and blood
Preparing body, mind and soul to be understood.

1940, midst World War II
A new life has begun really not much to do
Limited choices on its behalf
to leave Mom's womb
Temperature change, cold hands, bright room.

Defenseless, dependent on
mothers' hands of comfort
Unclothed, frightened, sounds unaware to sort
Nature has not totally created a
sense of comfort, just cry
Radical sudden changes, cared
for by Mom, not to die.

Soon caring souls brought warm dry relief
Diapers, milk, Mom's supported hug was so brief

Nurse's watchful eyes scan small body stress

Weigh scales determine what is more or less.

One short week in big city done

Boarding a steam train, rails taking me home

Horse drawn buggy brought comforting air

Old mud house, I was carried in on a dare.

—DENNIS H. HOYER

Meeting God: My Real Talk with God

After selling my house in Wildwood and packing up with the U-Haul, I had to stop at a nearby small town to sign all legal papers for the sale of the land. It was about 2:00 p.m. There was not a cloud in the sky. It was 25 degrees with no wind. The truck was on the parking lot while I was talking to the lawyer.

Now get this, I left the lawyer's office and got in the cab of the truck and sat down to go to Maple Creek.

This is no lying about any of the following. The sky turned back. There was a hurricane wind, torrents of rain, smashing hailstones, thunder and lightning. There was no other thought than that the world would end. However, I had absolutely no fear of anything as I was hanging onto the steering wheel, lying on the seat of the truck, being tossed about.

Now this is what God spoke to me. "Dennis, I have followed you all your life. I told you many things, but you did not listen. Now hear this. From this point, you will do exactly what I say. You have absolutely nothing to say, and I am going to take full control of your life, and you will not have any choice in this matter.

The storm left as if nothing had happened. It went back to normal sunshine. And that is the way it has been ever since. Praise Jesus. Amen.

The next day, arriving in Maple Creek, I parked the truck in the back yard. I laid my hands on my property, every square inch of it. Then I did the same in the house. I vowed there would never be an argument in the house, and at this point, after 9 years, there has not been one.

2007 Breaking My Leg at the Ranch

I was helping my friend on the ranch, repairing a feed silo. Those silos held 100 truckloads of silage used to feed cattle in the wintertime. In the silo, there is a machine called an unloader. It is used to dig the silage out of the silo to feed animals. The unloader was disconnected and pulled out of the silo. Because the unloader had to be taken out of the barn to be repaired, it had to be chained to the tractor.

Now chained to the bucket, the unloader was lifted up to be removed to the outside through the overhead door. This unloader is 3' x 3' x 30' and weighs 7000 lbs.

While backing the tractor out of the shed with the unloader, I grabbed the chain to turn the unloader a bit to get it through the door. The chain slipped off of the hook, falling to the ground. Well, it fell on my leg and broke it.

While lying on the shed floor in pain, waiting for the ambulance to take me to the hospital, I observed angels floating above me. They appeared to be coming out of the walls and floating around.

The angels appeared in transparent rainbow colors. They were so beautiful and soothing. It really was a Heavenly experience.

Drinking Spring Water at a Ranch

A month after arriving at Maple Creek, I was walking down the street when a rancher stopped to say hi. He said, "Hello, Dennis. I am going back out to my ranch, so jump in, and I will take you out and show you my ranch." Upon arriving at the ranch, he took me out to the pasture. We walked among a herd of cattle. He advised me to lay down in the grass with him. There was a spring coming up from the ground. We both lay in the grass drinking this cool clear water like a couple of kids. It was the best drink of water I have ever had.

2008: Vision While Praying in Tongues

A few years ago I attended a full gospel men's retreat in the Cypress Hill Resort Inn. There were approximately one hundred men attending. The entertainment was speakers and music. The worship continued for some time. Towards the end of the service, they then called for prayer.

Only a few moments later, the call came inviting the Holy Spirit to come and take over.

We all worshiped in tongues, one-half to three-quarters of an hour.

When I was worshipping in the Spirit, a vision appeared of Jesus on the Cross.

I sat down on a chair and wrote the following poem. Praise the Lord. Amen.

The Appearing of the Mighty Cross

The mighty Cross appeared against a crystal sky

A piercing rising sun blazed brilliantly beyond

Creating a mystical shadow toward me

Wisdom revelation and truth

created for me a bond

Your almighty power was revealed

Jesus you left and you are not there

You have come down off of the wood

Now you are living in me for others to share

Vividly and blameless it rose from the ground

Heavenward my hungry eyes humbly gazed

Between God and me it firmly stood

Death talk no longer will be raised

Promises for the day were sealed forever

Lord you took and finished the place of sin

For a very brief moment there was darkness

Now a new life without regret will begin

—DENNIS H. HOYER

My Personal Viewpoint

The police uniform gives the same reaction as the Cross.

I have learned and understand some things and not some things. I understand that I do not understand.

Even when I was not a Christian, but wearing the police uniform, people would look at me with mixed emotions – some surprised, some fearful and/or threatened.

Now as a Christian, people have told me to leave lots of times, yelling at me and saying, "Get out of here. I am living in hell, and I am going there. I do not want any of your crap."

I had not said a word or done anything to them.

Yet, we as Christians are to live in the light of the world. People in the darkness unconsciously see that light in the way we live. Praise the Lord.

Two snails persevered to get on the ark!!

Chapter Nine:
Mission Trips

Mexico Mission Trip – 2010

For three months, I took my van camper down to Vicente Guerrero, Mexico, which is south of San Diego, on the Baja of California.

I needed some dental work done and some glasses at a border town called Algodonas, Mexico, which is just outside of Yuma, Arizona. I stayed there for a few days to rest up and soak up some of the sun.

While in Yuma, at 5 a.m., I went to a McDonald's outlet for breakfast. Upon entering the restaurant, I observed a homeless person sleeping in a corner booth. I sat down on the other side of the table and poked him. I asked him if he wanted coffee and ham and eggs. "Oh sure" was the reply. While eating breakfast, he pulled out a tattered old Bible. It seemed that he knew it by heart. Boy, did I ever get some wonderful sermons. It was amazing.

I asked him where he had spent the night. "Oh, down on the sidewalk in front of the bank. It sure was cold last night." I asked him where his sleeping bag was. "Well, my friend lost his bag so I gave him mine because he was cold." Oh my God, talk about being speechless!!!

I took him to the mall and bought him a sleeping bag. I got the best hug of my life. My God is So Good. Amen.

Now I had to go into Algodonas, Mexico, across the border to get my glasses. While getting my glasses filled, I was sitting on a roller chair on a brick floor. The lady that was fitting my glasses spoke some broken English. She was a very nice lady.

Now the whole shop, which was full of people, started to tremble. I thought I was going to puke because of an upset stomach. Yes, it really got bad. Now all the building were shaking, twisting, and turning. Everyone was scrambling to get outside. Glass shelves full of eyeglasses crashed to the floor. Broken glass was scattered all over tiles on the floor. The marble tiles were about 18" x 18". These tiles had heaved in the middle and were standing on edge. There were the weirdest sounds I have ever heard. Before this all started taking place, I was sitting on a chair with castors on it. The racket was supersonic. It lifted me up and hurled me in to the wall. There I was on the floor. I peered up in all directions in a daze. There was dust all around. The people were in terror, all screaming in Spanish at me from the outside to get out of the building. I could not understand them. There was rubble from wall to wall. I got up onto my feet in a daze.

All seemed to settle down. I was standing there saying to myself, "Where is my van. I am a hay seed from Saskatchewan and have no idea what is going on here."

It was so crazy. All those tiles in the floor were almost all back in place where they originally had been. People were starting to come back into the store to check things out.

I got my chair up and sat trying to assess what had happened. The lady that was fitting my glasses came to me and sat down in front of me, stunned, frazzled, crying, and unable to talk. Moments later she began talking. She was unable to finish fitting my glasses because she was too upset. I let her talk till she got her breath back. I talked a little with her. Then I reached in my pocket and got out a Spanish tract. She read it and I watched her expression change in her face. She accepted Jesus, sobbing, saying, "Thank you ever so much."

I went back in the USA bookstore, bought her a nice Spanish New Testament Bible, and went back. I got my glasses and gave her the Bible. I received another wonderful hug. Wow. Back at the border to get in the USA, there were four guys talking about their experience in the bar. One guy was waving his arms. I will never take another drink as long as I live!

The next day, the headline in the paper read: "7.9 earthquake hits Mexico".

2010 Joan Hunter in B.C. – 2010

On the way home from a Mexico mission trip, I drove up the west coast of the USA to Richmond, British Columbia. I stayed at a hotel where I found a healing seminar going on. It was being led by Joan Hunter's ministry out of Texas, USA.

This was a three-day event. I took in every minute of it as it all spoke to my heart. My dad, my son, and I have hip displacement. I had a doctor examine me twenty years ago. He told me that the only cure was hip replacement. He said when I was not able to function anymore, I was to come and see him.

Now because of all the heavy long hours of the mission trip, my hip gave up. Upon coming to the healing seminar, I was barely able to walk, sit, or stand. Really, I was prepared now for hip surgery when I got home.

After two days at the seminar, I got up to the stage to see Joan for healing. As I came to her, she asked me what problem I had. I told her I was going for hip surgery when I got home because of the pain. Joan said, "I want you to walk across the stage." I walked maybe fifteen feet when she said, "Stop and turn around." I turned around. I felt and heard a squishing sound. Joan said, "How is that?"

I replied, "The pain is gone." Joan asked if there was anything else. I thought for a second. I did not want to ask God for two things, but I asked anyways. With my right hand pointed to the right side of my neck, she said, "Pain be gone. It is completed." By the time I touched my neck, the pain was gone.

Joan asked again if there was anything else. I said, "No, I had just met the real surgeon, Jesus." I had received a new hip.

The next day, the ministry moved to another town in a school gym. I followed them.

This is what happened. There was a man that was pushed through the back door in a wheelchair by his family. This man was very angry and calling Joan names from the middle of the gym floor. Joan came off of the stage. This man began screaming at her saying he did not want prayer.

Joan asked him why he came here then. He said his family had picked him up and brought him there. Joan said, "Okay, but you cannot stop me from praying for you." She did from a distance. The man left.

The next night he came back again. He rolled up to the stage, apologizing, and then asked for prayer. Joan had two men on her team take him off to the corner to pray for him.

The next thing I saw, this man was out of his wheelchair. In the wheelchair was one of the praying men. He then pushed the man around the gym. I have a photo of that. Thank you, Jesus. Amen.

This is another story while at the same meeting. One lady, who was about 25 years of age, came with a friend in crutches. She had been a jogger, and all she ever wished was to be able to jog again.

Another mid-aged lady came to the front with crutches. Her only wish was to climb stairs after a car accident she had been in.

Another lady came with no teeth. All she wanted was teeth, which she was not able to pay for. Her family had been poor when she was a child. Her parents pulled her teeth as a child because they never had money to repair them.

Guess God had all this all set up for my benefit. I happened to be sitting beside a retired Mission dentist. He stood up and stated she was to come to his office. He gave her his card, saying, "I will replace your teeth."

The anointing and the power of God hit. I was on the floor just howling. Joan shut the meeting down until I started coming around.

As I was getting to my feet, I heard a lady screaming as she ran up and down the stairs. The other lady went jogging with her friend. They both were sweaty from running.

Thank you, Jesus. Amen.

Many years ago, I took training through a Lutheran church, which gave me Stephen minister credentials.

I now follow Joan Hunter around in Western Canada and Haiti as time and funds provide.

I pray for people almost every day. I personally could write a book about my own experiences.

I continue to listen to God and to do what he tells me to do. Amen.

Joan Hunter has been my mentor. She gave me the chance and also trusts me. Joan's testimony has encouraged me to write this book.

Thank you, Jesus. Amen.

Cowboy Brett – 2010

On my way to Mexico on a mission trip with my camper in 2010, I was doing some touring and sightseeing in the Palm Springs area of the United States. In the dessert, I spotted an old building of some sort about a half a mile away. I stopped to gaze and daydream.

That night in the dessert I envisioned an old movie scene of Old West gunfights, bandits, and brawling on the streets. I wrote the following poem. I found it very exciting to allow my mind to just fly in all directions. So here it is. Enjoy.

Cowboy Brett

Mid-August doggies, herded, to lush green grass

Mountain brook, brings cool water to drink

Fencing, branding chores all complete

Proudly gazing over shady ranch

Brett begins to think

Life is passing by, time for a change

Haggard restless, I think I'll wander to town

Adventure was absent, in his young life

Tomorrow is the day, to a man I have grown

Four; thirty saddled up, neck reined to left

Birch trees shimmering, their silver dress

Cobble-stoned brook, hoofs

clattering stirring sand

Good-bye to his herd, feeling some stress

Star pitted sky, was lifting veil of darkness

Birds begin welcoming warmth, this fresh day

Breeze causing waves in his tattered beard

Reality now set in, while checking his pay

Riding over a ridge, towards a grove of spruce

There appeared his friend, Roppin' Joe

Greetings are shared, hi with a firm handshake

Chewing off a plug saying good-

bye, would curl his toe

High noon, town structures now appear

Wide sandy streets many folk strolling about

Horse in stable, now wide-eyed,

this adventure is real

Loud music dancing, whisky

odder, create some doubt

Beyond noisy hard wood floor

pretty ladies at the bar

After a few snorts of liquid corn,

he is feeling his place

Old time fiddling contest was

on, oh how nice this is

Heading for a bath, Brett pinched

a lady, with no grace

Only seconds passed when the

grip of a rustler felt

Tables crashing, through swing-

ing door, face with dirt did meet

Pain was abound in groin, including rear end

Now plans are changing, while gathering his feet

I just do not fit here, being hillbilly and all

Dusting his jeans with cowboy

hat, this I do not need

Counting his blessings at the undertaker's door

Hustling towards his horse, that

had not eaten his feed

Shortly Brett was back on the range

Licking his wounds, his saddle under his head

Rising moon brought harmony, for

all nature's mating songs

His creator advised, this really is my bead.

—DENNIS H. HOYER

5:00 a.m. Call to Be with a Dying Man – 2011

It was 5:00 a.m. in Maple Creek. A caregiver called me to the house of a 90-year-old man who was dying. Upon entering the house, there was this man, his wife, and a caregiver. She showed me to a 90-year-old man. This person was lying on a stretcher bed by a patio, overlooking the lawn outside.

I pulled up a chair beside the bed and started talking to this man.

He was gasping for air. His skin and bones were frail, and he was unable to talk.

Not able to do anything, I grabbed his hand and prayed silently. The caregiver advised me that he was not a Christian.

As this man was struggling and gasping for air, his hand came up and down with my hand.

After three hours I started talking to him. I carefully explained the Cross to him. I explained the difference between Heaven and Hell and how to get to Heaven. I was aware that he was not able to talk about what I had told him. I prayed over him. I told him that he was to squeeze my hand if he understood. I recited the sinner's prayer aloud. I then asked if he understood the story of Jesus and that he was loved. I told him that if he believed the story of Jesus, he should squeeze my hand.

He squeezed hard. His hand and arm fell limp. He had gone home to be with the Lord.

Haiti Mission – 2012

After being around Joan Hunter at different Canadian locations, there was a God orientated learning curve in the works. Listening to Joan's testimony and being a part of the healing ministry environment caused a stir in my life. Joan trusts me and permits me to work alongside her during the services.

In 2012, the opportunity arose to travel to Haiti with Joan Hunter for a week. Our team ministered at a church that held a 1000 people. Services last usually 3 to 4 hours, morning and night.

I could write a book on the subject of that experience alone. After watching the Haiti people worshiping for a couple of hours, our team of 27 went in amongst the crowd to do ministry.

Standing amongst the people, not knowing the language, I had absolutely no idea of what to do next.

I asked God what I should do. I started to praise the Lord and singing in tongues. There was a young lady coming towards me holding her throat indicating for me to heal her. I raised my hand saying IN THE NAME OF JESUS. She was overcome with such an enthusiasm and passion for her Lord that she buckled and fell to the floor bathed in God's love. The rest was history. The service went on to the wee hours of the morning.

Dream of Jesus – 2012

One night while sleeping in my bed, at 72 years of age, I had this dream or vision appear to me. I was in a log cabin, standing on the side of a roughly 40' x 30' building. I must explain that all this is a scene that my earthly words are not able to describe and do it justice.

At the other end of the room stood Jesus in a dazzling, glittery, white cloak or robe. I was not able to see His face clearly, but there was no doubt it was He.

There were no words spoken.

The inside of the magnificent building and its spectacular decor are very difficult to describe. The ceiling was made of very dark eloquent logs, and the magnificent walls surrounded you to make you feel warm and comfortable.

There was no fear or concern while standing there. I just wanted to look at Him. His hands were at His side, straight down. However, His open palms were extended towards me. Instantly, I felt I was lifted up and was floating towards Him. Nearing Him, I passed right through His perfect robe and I found myself standing at the back of him. That was a Holy experience as I felt His cleansing power and redemption.

Mexico Trip – 2015

During the past eight years, I have gone to Mexico once on a house build. Another time I went down there in my camper van. That was in 2010 for three months. While down there, I had the opportunity to meet and get close to some special people. Also I was water baptized in a large church.

In December 2014, I had a vision of being at a large church doing a healing service among the Mexican community.

In the last couple of years, it seems that the Lord speaks to me in vision and dreams at around 3 a.m.

My thoughts over the past year had been perhaps to go back to Haiti, but not to Mexico. Now the dream about Mexico had to be dealt with.

One thing led to another. The plans were made to go on a house build mission to Mexico with a group of 26 people from this area.

I spoke to the leader of the team about the mission plans and my dream or vision. I told the leader that I would help with the house build, however, my focus was to pray for the people.

Now I e-mailed my friend in Mexico and explained in English about my vision and plans. His reply came back in scrambled English. My friend stated he had two churches for me to speak at, plus was talking to another and a Detox Centre.

My friend's reply in broken English ended with, "You come down here and we will juice it up."

After three days of travelling in two vans plus two half-tons, we arrived at our destination. Once there, we attended the Sunday evening church service. That church was the one that my vision had been about. Well, it was a very spiritual service, but I did not speak.

On the third day of the mission, I went to a church out in a field. It was a tent building 20' x 30'. There were a few chairs on the dirt floor, with a plastic tarp over it. There were people crowded outside. Inside, it was packed tight with people. I spoke for about 10 minutes. Three ladies knelt on the dirt floor by a small pulpit. They were all crying and wanting prayer. My friend was doing the interpreting as I prayed over those three ladies in English and in tongues. They seemed very happy. After that, the outside people prayed for our team. It was very special, with a lot of prayer and Holy Ghost activity taking place. The next day at 6 a.m., I spoke at the Alcohol Treatment Centre with 30 men. Because there were only men and no children, my testimony was about my drinking career. The response was really heartwarming. I held nothing back.

On the sixth day was an evening service. I spent the whole day in prayer and preparing my talk. I was mainly praying that at this upcoming service God would remove all of "me" in the service – my pride, humanness, etc. I wanted only what He wanted to be said and what would be done.

The service was at 7:00 p.m. at a newly built church, 15 miles south of our little town. We took 10 people from our team along with care packages of oil, rice, beans, toiletries, etc.

It was 6:45 p.m., and I was sitting in the front row with a lady member of our team and with no other people in the church. I was crying.

I was crying about how God had brought me to Mexico to do healing ministry. I believed that had to be a supernatural miracle.

At 6:55 p.m. there were still were no people in the church. My friend played a couple of praise songs. I walked up on the stage. I turned around and the place was packed. At least 100 people plus many outside. I spoke no more than 5 minutes. The house came down. People were coming down to the stage for healing, jamming in close. I said to my friend, "We have to stop preaching and get praying." Many of the team became involved in praying for others. We prayed for two hours.

The Holy Ghost hit with the anointed Spirit of God. This part I learned after the service. There were boys 19 to 20 years of age outside heckling the service in the church. Three people saw them. At that point I was still preaching. They all jerked their heads over towards the front of the church. They fought their way down the side of the wall among the people. My friend met them by the side of stage. All five gave their hearts to the Lord that evening. Not one of them had ever been in a church before.

Revelation from a Child – 2015

I was watching a movie about an 8-year-old child running into her mother's arms for comfort to still the fear she had been feeling.

As a child, I had never entertained the idea that I would be able to go to a human being with a situation or problem. I always was so wrong. No matter what I thought or did, it was wrong. When going to my mother for anything, I knew I would get beat up, and I believed I deserved it. My belief was that if I did not get a beating, I deserved it anyway, and I wondered why I had not received it.

Never as an adult would I trust anyone that I did not know; nor did I know how to ask for understanding or receive it.

Throughout my life, I always felt guilty about being alive, believing I was the most ugly and stupid person in the world. I was never able to trust anyone. I thought that others were out to get me because I was weak. I had a "poor me" attitude. I was angry, alone, worthless, defeated, and unlovable. People did not understand me. I had the attitude that I would fix it and show them all that they were wrong, and that I would get over it. Most of my decisions were wrong, and I knew right from wrong. I chose wrong. But now I can represent Christ in my new life.

I can now enjoy myself. With all our imperfections and failures, it is no surprise to God that we are on the road we are travelling.

I still have to hear the message of Jesus to be sure that it is the right and true way. I have to trust it through faith, mercy, and grace.

Chapter Ten:
Stories that Are Dear to My Heart

These are just stories of some encounters I have had with people, as well as stories that have been told to me, that I believe are worth sharing. I have also included some scriptures that are particularly meaningful to me.

1915 Prairie Blizzard in Pinkie, Saskatchewan

(This was written by some relatives during the First World War. No editing has been done to keep it as it came to me.)

This winter of wartime was like other winters. High drifts of snow where it could find places to lodge, and our kitchen porch was one, high as the roof of the porch and filled in as high to the barn which was 150 yards away, with a granary with winter's supply of coal in it. We had two very large scuttles for coal that would last the day, and in the evening I would drag them out to the granary to meet brother Jack who was in his young teens, 14. It had been blowing two full days and nights, and Jack had cut steps in the snow bank so that we could get up and down. It was still blowing, but the drift was so high that we didn't feel it was going over the top of the kitchen. I was sure I could get to the granary so brother Jack could fill them up and bring them in for the night fuel.

I got my heavy extra clothes on, quite anxious to get out there before Jack would miss me. These were big scuttles, and I ran into trouble first at the snow steps. To me they were just plain stubborn, catching on the sides of the snow steps. I got to the top, raised my head above the rim of the drift, a different handicap. Well, I must get to the coal granary to meet Jack. Getting them up over the rim of the drift and climbing up myself, keeping control of the scuttles, now, I mean like right now, they became like open parachutes.

That 60-80 mile blizzard wind swept us completely across the snowdrift, yanking and yanking at my scuttles, like that is what it waited for all day, just to get rid of the scuttles once and for all. But my fingers were not that bad with rheumatism, the arm and leg cords were useless in this wind. The small metal handles let my fingers grasp right around them and I hung on, not knowing where it was going to stop. Not even thinking, it whipped me along on my belly like it knew all along what it was going to do with me, quite decided. When all of a sudden, we came to a stop, parachute scuttles and I. The blizzard was still trying very hard to get my scuttles out of my hands. Well luck was with me; the snow bank had not covered the top strand of barbed wire of a six-foot barbwire fence. One scuttle went under it, the other went over it, and I was holding on to both with the barbed wire giving my face an idea of what it thought of having any flesh rubbed up to it in freezing weather, then the storm dropped.

Right close to me, when I opened my eyes, was brother Jack. As he took the handles out of my hand, his first words were, "Why didn't you let them go?" My answer only a God-knowing boy could answer, in an 80-mile-an-hour blizzard with a mother and a coal stove depending on him, trying to act some bit grown up, with four older brothers wearing uniforms, "I would do as much as I could." Brother Jack's words to me, "You're still a kid with heavy winter clothes on." Love hadn't quite entered my pain-stricken body. Maybe when pain leaves, love and its full meaning will come back in a summertime or two, now it was still wood alcohol and cotton batten bandages.

A Touching Heroic Story

This story is from a man telling his childhood recollection of living in a house that was covered with 15 feet of snow. He was suffering with a severe case of arthritis. Digging up to the surface to the blizzard outside, he poked his head out of the snow bank with two empty coal pails. His intention was to get enough coal to survive the cold winter night. The wind blew him across the snowdrift and into a fence, but he would not let go of the pails although his hands were freezing.

While doing so, he was found hanging on to the coal pails, praying. An older brother found him. When asked why he never let the pails go, he replied, "I have four brothers overseas fighting for our country. Mom needed the coal to keep the house warm for the night. I just want to do my part." (What a hero!!!)

Police Stories

While on duty on a quiet Sunday afternoon, I decided to park my police car in an open field. After walking for roughly ten minutes, I came over a slight incline and took note of a parked car. Upon approaching the vehicle, I observed all the windows turned down. The motor was off, and no one around. Looking in the car, I saw a male and a female lying on the front seat. They were stark naked having sex. This was just too hard to resist. I pulled my 18-inch K light out, reached into the car, and poked the man on his butt. Oh yes, there was a lot of screaming and hollering with a lot of commotion. My Sunday afternoon stroll had become quite the event.

***

I attended a scene where a dog had gotten run over by a car and killed. I treated the scene very causally while trying to be sensitive to the owner. I was disciplined by the police brass and the mayor because my attitude was not caring enough in this situation. I learned and now know that when a pet gets killed, in most cases, it is more dramatic than when a person gets injured or killed.

***

One time at 4:00 a.m., just for something to do, I stopped to check out an abandoned car on the street. I was half asleep. The foolish thing was that I looked in the back seat though an open window with a flashlight. I observed a small, 6-inch square box lying on the far side of the rear seat. I crawled in the rear passenger's side window instead of going around to the driver's side. I reached in attempting to move the box to see what it was. I was not able to reach it. So I stretched and half crawled in the window to complete my investigation. Now get this. There was not a sound around at this time of night. It was extremely quiet. Extended to the max, I pushed the box with my flashlight.

Well, the box was one of those laughing boxes. Now there were some awful loud noises coming from that box. Me trying to get out of that window would have been one of the world's funniest videos.

***

On a rainy, cold, windy night, I was called out to a two-car crash. An elderly lady was in the passenger side of the car. She was partially conscious and had her leg crushed under the dash. The roof was torn off. She was moaning and groaning. There was a child, about

10 years old, unconscious and lying across the back seat that was covered with broken glass. No drivers around. Four policemen, six emergency firemen, plus two ambulance drivers were attending the scene. We were all cutting the car in pieces to get the lady out. As we started to pull the lady out, she was coming in and out of shock and really screaming. At this point, the husband came on the scene as he had been knocked out and had walked away. He saw all the commotion and jumped on our backs and started beating us. What a scene! The lady died a day later.

***

One afternoon, I was dispatched to a location about a dog fight. It was about -35° below. There was a pack of stray dogs on the loose. As I arrived on the scene, four dogs ran away in the deep snow, leaving behind a smaller dog that was really chewed up. I checked the injured dog and pronounced him dead. I called the city to send out a truck to pick up the dead dog.

The city did that. The driver stated he would drop the dog off at the incinerator on his way to lunch.

I was not able to find the owner of the dog.

Approximately one hour later, while having my lunch at the police station, someone called in to report a lost dog. I was paged to speak to the owner of the dog. She just happened to be a matron at the police office.

I went back to her house; she was crying about her dog. While talking to her I realized that it had been her dog that had been attacked and killed. She demanded to see her dog to say good-bye, even if it was already dead. Now what? I called the dispatch. I called the city and spoke to the driver who had attended to the dog fight. Fortunately, they had happened to go for lunch before getting rid of the dead dog. They came to the owner's house. The drivers opened the back doors to where the dog was lying. The lady looked in the back of the truck, called the dog's name, and the dog got up and ran to the lady and licked her face. The city guys and I just about died. From that moment on, I was a hero for years to come.

***

One night, at 3:00 a.m., I was dispatched to an address because a lady in Vancouver stated she had been unable to contact her dad for three days.

I walked around the house a couple of times trying to get in. Finally, with my flashlight I saw something moving on the living room floor. We got permission to break in. The old man had fallen out of his wheelchair and was trying to get up. What a mess; there was excrement, urine, etc. We got him to the hospital.

***

One afternoon I picked up some fried chicken to eat for lunch at the police station. I had booked out for lunch, but I received a call to go to a vehicle accident as there were no other cars on duty. When I got to the scene, there was a man and a motorcycle under a truck in the middle of the intersection. We pulled the bike out, and the man happened to be my son. He was scraped up, but okay. There were three witnesses there who told me my son had run a red light. I had to give him a traffic ticket for running a red light. While giving him his ticket, he ate my chicken. He still loves me.

***

The following is a true story and a real inter-departmental memo. This is just one example of the fooling around us cops did in our dull moments.

INTER-DEPARTMENTAL MEMORANDUM

Date and Time
FILE No. of This Memo
September 27th, 1993 2000hrs
A4229

FROM Cst. D.H. HOYER #202
TO Deputy Chief M. LANGGARD
SUBJECT Damage to Car 16 and to CST. D. KOCH. (RADIO)

SIR:
As a member of the police service with 24 1/2 years' experience I AM SECOND IN CHARGE AND SOMETIMES IN CHARGE. This task is a large undertaking and responsibility. The detention area includes sally port safety, police member safety, and disease

control. During my tour of duty I must monitor all life-threatening situations.

Issue #1

At the time of these two incidents in question during my hours of duty, I was on a highly sensitive mission that was to capture and destroy ill ants that could infect and cause sickness to prisoners and police members.

My function was to run water through the sally port area in order to attract the infected ants. While the water runs to the drain hold, plus with my careful encouragement with a sheet of plywood, the sick ants would get on the currant and down the sewer trap they would go. Then I pounce on the drain hole and cover same with the sheet of plywood. With this measure the problem is eliminated and peace is restored.

Cst. Walton, in my opinion, caused a diversion in the water flow by driving by with a police vehicle over the stream, causing the ants to divert and me being the one to be placed in an unsafe position of being chewed up by an ill ant. Cst. Walton should be warned about his careless behaviour that may cause injury to fellow brothers.

Issue #2 Re: radio of Cst. Koch

The other part of my responsibilities is to examine all police vehicles leaving the detention area for ill ants. When a highly sensitive operation is underway, I must at all times think of my fellow brothers' safety. As I was examining Cst. Callender and Cst. Koch's police vehicle for potential dangerous ants, Cst. Koch very quickly rolled down the passenger window in a hysterical manner. I very quickly got alarmed and thought that because of his very large nose and his fang (buck type) teeth just a glaring, that he may have been bitten by a rabid ant. I responded by throwing water at the immediate and surrounding area to prevent further injury to Cst. Koch's face. I believe Cst. Koch should also be talked to when an operation is in progress. He should stay in his police car and be silent.

Cst. D. HOYER #202

The Greatest Man

The Greatest Man in history is Jesus.

He had no servants, yet they called Him Master.

He had no degree, yet they called Him Teacher.

He had no medicines, yet they called Him Healer.

He had no army, yet kings feared Him.

He won no military battles, yet

He conquered the world.

He committed no crime, yet they crucified Him.

He was buried in a tomb, yet He lives today.

—Anonymous

Scriptures that Have Touched My Heart

Raising people from the dead

Luke 7:22, 23

"…the blind see, the lame walk, the lepers
are cured, the deaf hear, the dead are raised
to life, and Good News is being preached
to the poor. And tell him, God blesses those
who not turn away because of me."

John 6:39

"And this is the will of God, that I should not
lose even one of all those he has given me, but
that I should raise them up on the last day."

Acts 2:32

"God raised Jesus from the dead and
we are all witnesses to this."
(I have been raised from the dead).
God hates discord within the
brethren. It is TOXIC.
The story of my heart, it is the heart of my life.
I am done! I need to be rescued!

Reasons people do not get healed: Deliberate active UNBELIEF

Mathew 13:58

"And so He did only a few miracles
there because of their unbelief."

Mark 9:24

"The father cried out, "I do believe, but
help me overcome my unbelief."

Mark 16:14

"Still later He appeared to the eleven Disciples,
as they were eating together. He rebuked
them for their stubborn unbelief because they
refused to believe those who had seen Him,
after He had been raised for the dead."

Romans 11:23

"And if the people of Israel turn from their
unbelief, they will be grafted in again, for God
has the power to graft them back into the tree."

1 Timothy 1:13

"Even though I used to blaspheme the name of Christ, in my insolence, I persecuted His people. But God has mercy on me because I did it in ignorance and unbelief."

Hebrews 3:19

"So we see that because of their unbelief, they were not able to enter in His rest."

Math 13:54-57

"…They scoffed Him because He was only a carpenter… They were deeply offended and refused to believe in HIM."

MARK 16:16-18

"Anyone who believes and is baptized, will be saved. But anyone who refuses to believe will be condemned. These miraculous signs will accompany those who believe. They will cast out demons in my name, and they will speak in new languages. They will be able to handle snakes with safety, and if they

drink anything poisonous, it won't hurt
them. They will be able to place their hands
on the sick, and they will be healed."

Peter's Sermon

Peter is the priest at the Anglican Church that I attend. He is my spiritual mentor. I respect and honor his wisdom. The following is a sermon that he gave that was of particularly encouraging to me.

1 John 5:1-6

May only the truth be spoken here, may
only the truth be heard here. Amen.

The reading from the epistle today is hard to hear and full of challenges for us. A true understanding of the importance of the words and familiar terms that are in it will help us to understand what is being said and what action we need to take.

The first word that needs to be explained is "believe". "Believe" is one of those words that we all have come to a personal understanding about as we have lived in the world and been challenged to look beyond the obvious physical surroundings we live in, into the things that we believe that are beyond our experience. There are several words in the Greek that describe "believe". Some of them mean "sort of agree with" or "accept for the most part." Many people "believe" like that.

Those words allow us to believe but allow us to withhold our total commitment until it has been proved, and we can then claim that that was what we thought all along. Keeping our options open because we have a lack of trust in what we truly believe and allowing us to turn round at a later point and say in our defense, "Well, I said I believed, but I was never really committed to what I believed because I still had my doubts and besides I didn't want to make the changes necessary in my life that would prove I was fully committed to that belief." This is known as double mindedness and it has never convinced anyone on earth; so why would we expect it to convince God who is all-knowing, present everywhere, and all-powerful.

But St. John did not use those words when he wrote about 'believe.' He used a word that is exact and has no wiggle room attached to it. He used a word that means "really, totally, change-your-life-completely-believe". That is the type of belief that transforms the way we live and interact with others in this world. It screams loudly that we are God's children and we are intent on living out our earthly lives in that sure knowledge that we are His for all eternity. As a consequence, this world means nothing to us anymore because we clearly know that it is temporary and passing away. Nothing will remain of it. It will all pass away, and God will speak into existence a new creation where everything will be so real that it will last for eternity and not die or decay.

But we can only share in that new creation if we believe in a "really, totally, change-your-life-completely-believe" way. What we are called to believe is that Jesus is the Christ – the Son of God and that believing this totally, completely changes the way we live our lives in order to do what Jesus has asked us to do. Then we will be born again, but this time born of God, in the Spirit, through the water, and the blood of His Son Jesus Christ.

The second word that we need to better understand is "conquer". When we think of "conquer", we think of winning the war, causing our opponents to submit to our rule. In a personal sense, we think of how we have been successful in working within or outside "the system" to make a living for ourselves and to do well – judged by such things as having a home, enough to eat, heat in the winter, coolness in the summer, or the wealth to provide the type of life we want to live. When we have these things or any other specifics we have decided are essential, we consider ourselves conquerors and rulers of our domain. We are content and at peace.

But "conquer" means so much more – the Latin from which it came means to "completely gain or win – overcoming and taking control of a problem or weakness and gaining love, admiration, and respect". If what we completely gain or win is of this world, then we have gained nothing lasting. We have gained and won an illusion and given our life to it and thereby lost everything. No love, admiration, or respect in that, and we are still in our problem and displaying our weakness.

As one Christian colleague put it, "It's not what Satan offers us – it is what he takes away." All of Satan's armory is to deceive us into thinking we are in charge and is based around keeping us focused on the things of this world. As we heard only a few weeks ago, "What benefit is it to you if you gain the world and lose your soul?" We are deceived if we commit ourselves to the things of this world, and it will overcome us, leave us conquered, and in our problem and weakness.

Likewise, "it is what God offers to us and what that takes away that is most important." What God offers to us is that if we truly believe in Jesus as His Son, the Christ, He will adopt us as His children. We will be reborn in the Spirit, and we will be victorious in Christ overcoming Satan's power in this world to deceive, and ultimately, overcome death itself. Conquering in Christ that which we cannot conquer ourselves, gaining eternal life, removing our problem and our weakness and becoming true victors.

The third word we need to think about is "faith". We have gutted the word "faith.' We think that our "faith" is that we just say we are Anglican's – as if that says it all to someone seeking to understand what faith is. Sadly, that is generally enough these day because what "Anglican" means is lost in a tide of humanism and pluralism of the age we live in. It generally does not get challenged or asked to be clarified. We ourselves have some fuzzy idea that no matter how desperate things get out there in the world, and no matter how little we stand up for Jesus or proclaim His Kingdom, everything will always be fine for us here because we are able to keep the Anglican church doors open. Somehow we think that the true expression of our faith is that open Anglican Church doors means that our world remains conquered. We could not be more wrong. The entire scope of scripture from Genesis to Revelation is that God's people are always described as being in great conflict with the forces of evil that do not want us to really have faith in Jesus Christ as God's Son. God's whole "human experiment", if you want to call it that, was to prove that He could make a creature and give it true choice and it would choose to love Him even in the face of great temptation not to. The kind of faith that actively chooses the things of God instead of other things is the sort of faith that will conquer the world.

The world we are talking about is the world we refer to when in our baptismal covenant with God we vow to turn away from the world, the flesh, and the devil. Ouch! Please don't remind us that we made that contract with God. Too often we find that as St Paul said, "Our flesh wages war against the spirit." We find that we are often quite comfortable here in this world, and we prefer the company of other humans more than we do of God. We find that God's commandments that bring life are in fact contrary to the epistle, very burdensome, when we are very much of this world in our flesh, even if our spirit wants the things of God.

The truth here, of course, is that it is not our flesh that is weak, but rather that our spirits are not remembering the true strength of the faith we have – that it might be a small faith but it is in a great God and fully active when we believe in Jesus Christ as His Son who has overcome, conquered this world, the flesh, and the devil, and in him we are victors over them too. God gives us the power in Christ and His Spirit to resist the things of this world and become "over comers" and true "conquerors".

But St. John's statements that, "Everyone who believes that Jesus is the Christ has been born of God… and this is the victory that conquers the world, our faith," rests firmly on the understanding that what we believe means "really, totally, change-your-life-completely-believe". The type of belief that transforms the way we live and interact with others in this world. It depends upon understanding that to truly be victorious in conquering this world we have to reject the illusion of what Satan wants us to believe is conquering this world and put no value in the things of this world. Then we are truly gaining and winning life for eternity in the new creation with God.

All of this depends upon our faith being the kind of faith that actively chooses the things of God instead of other worldly things. This is the sort of faith that will conquer the world.

We cannot count ourselves among the victors – children of God, inheritors of the Kingdom to come, if we use our own earthly-based definitions of believe, conquer, and faith.

So now the rubber hits the road. A true test of what we believe, have conquered, and have faith in is whether we are willing to obey God's commandments or whether they are burdensome to us. From God's perspective, it should not be a burden for us believers to love the one who has adopted us as His own children, overcame the wiles of Satan, and defeated death for us; none of which we could do for ourselves even if we did have unlimited wealth or rule the earth. We, bathed in this amazing grace and love of God, should find no difficulty to love God and His other children and keep His commandments because they teach us how to live as His adopted children. If we cannot obey the commandments, love God and His children, and accept that we are more than victors in Christ – that we have conquered this world, I put it to you that you still have a problem with one of these three words – believe, conquer, and faith. Because we want to be our own god, these, if misunderstood, can cause you to gain the world – but lose your soul. Don't let that happen to you. (Used with permission from Rev. Peter Boote)

Chapter Eleven:
Someday...

Someday we will be standing in front of Jesus on Judgment Day, whether we believe it or not. Then the truth will be revealed to us, and there will no more negotiating. Philippians 2:10a, 11, NAS says, "That at the name of Jesus every knee should bow...and that every tongue should confess that Jesus Christ is Lord, to the Glory of God the Father."

When are we going to start living as if the Bible is true and alive?

We need to stop covering up our own guilt, shame, anger, bitterness, lack of forgiveness, resentment and hate. If we are lying to ourselves about our sins, healing will only begin when we get honest.

If we do not believe in forgiveness, we will not receive it.

In this life, by His grace and mercy, we are attempting to walk out what He has done on the Cross. Our unbelief works against faith (double-mindedness).

I have come to view death not as an end, but as a new beginning of life in our eternal home. This is where we will be united with many of our loved ones, those who accepted Christ as their Lord and Saviour.

I can face tomorrow because Jesus is alive. To me, this is faith, because faith is simply confidence in God.

Could it be that our difficulty in believing is holding us back from understanding how wonderful our tomorrow could be?

The storms of my life have determined my destiny. Anything I ask in Jesus' name, it shall be done. Amen.

My friend Jesus has totally forgiven all my sins and cleared my path for me to follow Him. Amen. This now is my purpose. Having come to know Jesus personally, God has placed His hand on me. This gives me a strong sense of assurance that I am the son of the Most High because of His mercy. Amen. This is for everyone. With God there is no respecter of persons. No sin is too bad for Him to forgive.

The enemy is after your/my future. "...Your adversary, the devil, prowls about like a roaring lion, seeking whom he may devour." 1 Peter 5:8a. NAS. "The thief comes only to steal, kill and destroy: I have come that they may have life, and have it to the full." John 10:10 NIV

As Christians we are to press in, rise up, live the abundant life, and seek restoration and more. As Christians we are "...to heal the sick, raise the dead, cleanse the lepers, cast out demons; freely you received, freely you give." Math 10:8 NAS "...they will lay hands on the sick and they shall recover." Mark 16:18c

As Christians, when we listen to God, His healing power is released through us. The quiet still voice of the Holy Spirit will speak to us as God uses us to pray for those in need.

We are to....

Push back sickness and disease

Speak words of encouragement

Revise, restore, and forgive

You are the breath of life. You call my name.

You Rescue me, Lord God. You are amazing.

You move mountains. You build us up.

We praise you, King of Glory.

You are faithful. You are truth.

Glory to your name.

I will follow you to eternity.

In the beginning, God spoke the word, and the heavens, the stars, and the universe came into existence,

I heard a speaker once who used the concept of a golf ball in relation to the earth. Just imagine God holding the whole world in His hands using the image of a golf ball. That is what it looks like in perspective from 350 million light years away in one of the many galaxies. Just imagine you on the golf ball. How big are you, really?

The next thing for you to imagine is God saying to you: "(Your name)...I have a plan for you. I love you.

I know every hair on your head. I will never leave you or forsake you." That's how important you are to God.

Since the beginning of time, man has chosen to separate himself from God through Sin. We humans are like the moon, which has no colour of its own. Our colour either reflects the glory of God, or it reflects the lies of the evil one. We need to share the love of God with even our worst enemy.

The wall of sin between God and us became so high, so thick, and so black, that we could not see over it, under it, or around it. That is why Jesus died on the Cross at Calvary (Because God loves all mankind). At the Cross as the veil ripped into two from top to bottom, people were washed from the graves and mercy and grace poured from the foot of the Cross out of Christ's love for us. This mercy and grace will never stop. It was then, it is now, and it will be here forever more for everyone.

When we meet Christ at the foot of the Cross, we enter into the circle of blessing where God abides. In that circle we have life in our spirit and body – life abundant and full. While there, we may begin to feel we are doing so well that we think, 'Oh, I am doing so well that I will just venture out a bit." Then you come back into the circle and then venture out again. Maybe a little farther next time, and before you know it, you are so far out that you begin to see the lies of the enemy as truth and your soul begins to lose the abundant life you had known before. God's word says that we need only ask Him to forgive us and He will send the Holy Spirit to reach out to us and lovingly guide us back to where God our Father resides in the centre of His circle of blessing.

So here is what you should consider. Close your eyes, bow your head, and imagine this scene…

You are lying in a grave under six feet of dirt. You may have a new pair of shoes on, a new suit or dress, and maybe some expensive jewellery…

Only remember that you will not be there. The body and everything in this world will return to dust. The soul lives on. You will be in heaven with Jesus or in hell with the devil (eternal darkness) for eternity.

Remember: Dead spirits don't move!!!!

Meaningful Wisdom

This is taken from the Alcohol Anonymous (Blue Book). It is a reading that really impacted my life, changing my attitude in regards to people, places and things during my treatment days.

'And acceptance is the answer to all my problems today. When I am disturbed, it is because I find some person, place, thing, or situation – some fact of my life – unacceptable to me, and I can find no serenity until I accept that person, place, thing, or situation as being exactly the way it is supposed to be at this moment. Nothing, absolutely nothing, happens in God's world by mistake. Until I could accept alcoholism, I could not stay sober. Unless I accept life completely on life's terms, I cannot be happy. I need to concentrate not so much on what needs to be changed in the world as on what needs to be changed in me and in my attitudes.'

(Used by permission from Alcoholics Anonymous, New York City, 1976)

These are some dreams and thoughts that I have collected throughout my life to place in my book of memoirs. I am happy to share them with you my readers:

- After a while you learn the difference between holding a hand and a caring soul
- You learn love does not hold security, you begin to learn kissed are not contracts
- Presents are not promises, you begin to accept your defeats with your head up and your eyes open
- With grace, not the grief of a child, you learn to build all your roads on today because tomorrow is too uncertain and futures have a way of falling down in mid flight
- When we risk sharing our real feelings, we develop relationships of understanding and trust
- For we cannot really care or be cared for, love or be loved, understood, unless we are willing to open our treasures of time, substance and self
- After a while you learn that even sunshine burns is you get too much
- So plant your own garden and decorate your own soul, instead of waiting for someone to bring you flowers
- I have learned I can endure. That I really am strong, I really have worth, and that God loves me so much

- And I learn and learn with every good bye. I learn and will keep learning.

(The previous information written on my heart, and I made it my Credo to live by.)

Dennis. "Thank You God."

How to Ask God into your life in preparation for Salvation, to give your life to Jesus and your ticket to Heaven and eternal life.

Now I am asking you to bow, kneel, lie down, sit on the toilet seat, or whatever. Speak to Jesus from your heart, with a faith that is beyond your own understanding. At that moment, the Holy Spirit will change your heart and your life from the inside out.

Now read the following prayer:

Sinner's Prayer

Heavenly Father, in Jesus' name

I ask you to forgive me of all my sin

Cleanse my heart and my life

I ask that everything I have ever said or done

Would be forgiven by the Blood of Jesus Christ

From this moment forward

I chose to serve Him

As my Lord and Savior

And now the angels of God

Are writing my name in the Lamb's Book of Life

I'm on my way to Heaven, and

the angels are rejoicing

In Jesus' name, Amen.

Having done this, seek out a true Bible-preaching church, a place where you can get involved in and become a part of a Bible study. Oh yes, pray lots in the name of Jesus, Amen.

Diagram of Changes Our Life Takes When We Walk with God

These are the changes in our life when we meet Jesus at the foot of the cross:

Sorrow	Joy
Hurt	Comfort
Worry	Peace
Grief	Joy
Confusion	Clarity
Sadness	Cheer
Worthlessness	Favour
Brokenness	Healing
Hate	Forgiveness
Persecution	Acceptance
Weakness	Power

Hell	Salvation
Resentment	Forgiveness
Disappointment	Contentment
Trauma	Relaxation
Pain	Relief
Strife	Peace
Loss	Reconciliation
Despondence	Hope
Sickness	Health
Stress	Relaxation
Death	Life
Dishonour	GloryBuild-up/Credibility

My parting words to you...

I have explained my life story to you the best way I know how. By the grace of God, my dream is that you will have gained a new perspective on life from the heart of a born-again, Spirit-filled Christian man. It was only Jesus who cleansed my heart and soul by shedding His blood on the Cross.

After leaving this earth, we will be with Jesus in glory, praising Jesus. No more pain, suffering, sorrow, no earthly thoughts. We will be filled with peace and joy beyond comprehension.

Remember, this will not happen if we do not receive Jesus as our Lord and Savior by believing that He came to earth, walked on it, preached to us from His living word, suffered, and died on the Cross paying the debt for all our sins. He did this freely and unconditionally for our Salvation, so that we would be in heaven with Him for eternity. He promised that He will do that because no matter what you have done, you are as pure as the white driven snow.

If you do not ask Him into your heart, you will not be with Him in Heaven. You will be in hell with the devil for eternity. The Bible says very few will make it, and the only thing that will hold you back is PRIDE. It is up to you to decide.

Sources of Information

I will mention that, over my lifetime, I have read a few books and watched plenty of Christian television, in addition to attending church. Most of my life I have carried a notebook and written down things that have touched my heart and soul. See my list below:

Alex Tresniowski	Joyce Meyers
Anthony Demello	Kris and Jason Corthsoul
Bill Gaither	Lee Strobel
Billy Graham	Lowell Lundstrom
Bill Wise	Maris Woodsworth Etter
Bruce Wilkerson	Mary K. Baxter
Charles and Francis Hunter	Max Lucado

Creflo Dollar

Crystal McVee

Dwight Mason

E.G. White

Elizabeth George

Faith Alive Family Church

F.F. Bosworth

Heaven is for Real

Jim Cymbala

Joan Hunter

Joel Osteen

John Eldridge

John Haggie

John G. Lake

Joseph Prince

Miracle Channel, Canada

Oswald Chambers

Pamela Jackson

Randy Alcorn

Reinhard Bonke

Rick Warren

Rev. Peter Boote

R.T. Randall

R.W. Schamback

Sid Roth

Smith Wigglesworth

Steven Furtick

T. L. Osborn

For more information or comments,
please visit my website:
www.dennishoyerrescued.com

About the Author

Dennis Hoyer is a born-again, spirit-filled believer. He was born in rural Saskatchewan and today lives with his wife Brenda in Maple Creek, the most "cowboy town" in Saskatchewan. Hoyer is a Stephan Minister and has gone on several mission trips to Mexico and Haiti. when not helping to spread the word, Hoyer enjoys playing the guitar, writing cowboy poetry, woodworking, restoring John Deere tractors, and having fun with his grandchildren. Hoyer says that since finding God, "my life has been a blast. Thank you, Jesus. Amen"

I have a place in Heaven

Please don't sing sad songs for me,
For get your grief and fears.
For I am in a perfect place,
Away from pain and tears.
I'm far away from hunger,
And hurt and want and pride,.
I have a place in Heaven,
with the master at my side.
My life on earth was very good,
As earthly lives can go,
But Paradise is so much more
Than anyone can know.....
My heart is filled with Happiness,
And sweet rejoicing, too.
To walk with God is perfect peace.
A joy forever new.

I have made a video to show at my funeral which states to those attending, "if you have not received Jesus Christ as your Lord and Savior, you will not be seeing me again." Amen

Printed in Canada